God's Angels Need No Wings

CLAUS WESTERMANN

God's Angels Need
No Wings

translated by
DAVID L. SCHEIDT

FORTRESS PRESS   PHILADELPHIA

This book is a translation of *Gottes Engel brauchen keine Flügel*, copyright © 1978 by Kreuz Verlag in Stuttgart, Germany.

Biblical quotations from the Revised Standard Version of the Bible, copyright 1946, 1952, © 1971, 1973 by the Division of Christian Education of the National Council of the Churches of Christ in the U.S.A., are used by permission.

ENGLISH TRANSLATION COPYRIGHT © 1979 BY FORTRESS PRESS

Library of Congress Cataloging in Publication Data

Westermann, Claus.
  God's angels need no wings.

  Translation of Gottes Engel brauchen keine Flügel.
  1. Angels. I. Title.
BT966.2.W4713   235′.3   78-14676
ISBN 0-8006-0535-7

7412K78   Printed in the United States of America   1–535

Contents

PART TWO

Preface

If someone were to ask me if I had ever seen an angel, I am afraid I could not give a very satisfying answer. But should I be asked if I have ever met a messenger of God, then the answer would be an emphatic and unequivocal, "Yes, I have!" Now, the Bible speaks about angels— better said, about God's messengers—not because it wants us to believe in angels as well as in God but rather so that God can draw nearer to us. The stories in the Bible that speak of angels relate the experiences of men and women to whom God drew so very near in moments of great personal crisis or danger that they sensed in the words of a human being the work of a messenger of God, and in the help of a human hand they felt the helping hand of God.

It has been quite some time since the first edition of this book was published in Germany. In those days I was just starting out as a teacher; now my teaching career is drawing to a close. I agreed to the republication of this book (and to its translation into English) because, it seems to me, we are still quite a long way from understanding and affirming what the Bible is saying when it speaks about angels. The fact that the Bible understands angels to be God's intimate way of speaking to and acting in the world means that the matter of angels is not a peripheral one. In fact, the subject of angels moves me today as much as it did when I wrote the first German edition, for those old Bible stories of encounters with God's messengers have their counterparts in our lives today, no matter where we are or what we may be doing. Indeed, these stories have preserved and handed down to us the experiences of ordinary men and women for whom a word from God or a crucial turning point in life came not in some supernatural or miraculous way but in and through the commonplace events of life, within the framework of everyday life and experience.

It is my sincere hope that this book will help its readers to think along the lines laid down in it. I am so bold as to hope that it will even help the reader to hear what the Bible has to say about angels with a sense of expectation.

CLAUS WESTERMANN

Part One

Messengers and the Message

> If angels no longer came to people, this world would go to pieces. As long as God sustains this earth he will send his angels.

> Angels are older than any and all religion. Indeed, they still come even to people who do not want to hear anything about religion.

What a blessing it is that angels do not concern themselves with what people think about them or even whether people believe in them. They cannot concern themselves with such matters because their entire existence is concerned solely with whatever task God has assigned them, what today is often called simply "mission." An angel is "born" for a certain task, and when that certain task is discharged, the angel ceases to exist as such. The whole sum and substance of an angel is to be a messenger who brings a message.

My purpose here is not to try to explain the nature of angelic existence. Frankly, I think it is good that we cannot do such a thing. It is rather my purpose to resist any attempt or inclination to conceive of angels in terms of human concepts.

If we listen carefully to how people speak of angels today, one thing stands out. People don't believe in angels anymore. They haven't believed in angels for centuries. And yet people speak of angels as though they do exist.

People speak of angels in a way similar to the way in which they speak of God. People will speak of God as long as the earth exists. And it is by no means only believers who will speak of God. We cannot replace God, yet we can replace the words we use to speak about God. We can even replace the name God itself. People will continue to speak about God, and they will speak even more about angels. You see, angels are God's possibilities; they give shape and form to God in his possibilities for us. What would this world be without such possibilities for us? We simply could not live without them. Life would have no meaning.

An angel is a messenger of God. But why does God need messengers? He doesn't really. Yet angels play a very important part in what God does; therefore, we can easily say that he needs them. When does God use a messenger? In ancient times the Greek armies needed a marathon runner, someone who ran more swiftly than all the rest, to carry the news of victory. But the commanders of the armies could not be that messenger. They had to stay at their posts. They could not at the same time be both commanders and messengers.

Further, the messenger had to be ready to go at a moment's notice. When we think along such lines as these, we can see why God sends angels.

The messengers during World War II—we called them dispatch runners—had something of the marathon runner about them, not because of the speed with which they carried their messages but because of the nature of their task. In the case of the marathon runner we are bound to ask, "Why did he run himself to death?" The fact is that there are messages of such import that the messenger can indeed run himself to death. Obviously, everything depends on the nature and importance of the message that needs to be carried. There are many such messages. And there are messages whose very nature calls forth the messengers to bear them.

The motorcycle dispatch riders of the last world war were needed in spite of the fact that other methods of communication were available. That is the case with God's angels. In theory there is no need for angels, because God is present everywhere. If God is present everywhere, then he does not need to send messengers. But he does send angels. It is precisely at the point where our human concepts of God can reach no further that the messages of angels begin.

In the case of God's angels the greatest distance is involved, and angels have to bridge the distance between God and humankind. This distance is what makes the message of angels necessary. We can express God's distance only in terms of space. The psalms ask why

God is so far off and entreat him to rise up, to draw near to us, to be attentive to us. Yet we know that these spatial concepts do not correspond to what we mean when we speak about God's being far off. If angels are God's messengers, then the idea of spatial distance is strengthened, for it is the function of a messenger to bridge a spatial distance.

But we cannot imagine how a messenger of God overcomes the distance between where God is and where people are. We cannot conceive of this, nor can we in any way portray it, because God's distance is not really a spatial one. So, then, we can say at the very outset that a concept or portrayal of angels which emphasizes the overcoming of spatial distance—for example, an angel with wings, to the extent that the wings are supposed to mean the putting aside of the distance between God and humankind—is not acceptable. When a messenger arrives we have no way of knowing what he brings. We must wait for him to speak. In our day messengers have become increasingly neutral. They do not just speak; they report. Today the opening and reading of a letter or the decoding of a message correspond to what antiquity called opening the mouth and speaking. With this speaking the apprehension and anxiety caused by the messenger's appearance end. Every genuine tension offers us the alternatives of saying yes or no, of woe or weal, freedom or nonfreedom, breathing easily or anxiety.

The marathon runner brought the good news of victory, but angels do not bring only good news. If God announced only good news he would be no god at all. The messengers of Job are a classic example of messengers who bear bad news. One must read the words of these messengers in Job 2 in all their vivid monotony. Genuine monotony is the echo of death or eternity. Boredom is a collapsed form of monotony.

The heaping of reports of bad news for Job which we find in that chapter also has a very subtle, completely hidden meaning to it. The serious-minded reader will say that these reports are exaggerated; but that is not the way it happened. "And behold, when he had spoken, there came another who said. . . . " Of course, this is a matter of literary style. This portrayal wants to indicate that there is a limit, a stopping point. The horizontal aspect of human existence can conceive of only so much misfortune. Once the bounds of this misfortune are exceeded, the person who has suffered so much reacts to what has befallen him with utter numbness and madness. But Job responds with the one thing that endures: the praise of the Lord who gives and who takes away. The praise of God is something that can raise thick walls of defense against encroaching meaninglessness. There is a difference between being overcome by misfortune and being told about it. Job stood his ground firmly in the face of the misfortunes that had been reported to him. Then illness struck him. Even this blow he parried. But then came that pointless, consuming plague, that long, torturous living death. Then Job's complaint began in earnest.

A message of impending misfortune always presumes

that there is in the person to whom such a message is directed some intact and untouched area. The announcement of a misfortune in advance presumes that the one to whom the announcement is made feels personally secure and free so that he can receive such a message and come to terms with it. Therein lies one thing that the announcement of good fortune and ill have in common: both are received in the same way. The moment in which one is expecting the message is one of a wavering between hope and fear. It is like that moment in which a judge begins pronouncement of sentence upon a convicted defendant. Perhaps good fortune and misfortune are alike in that moment in which a message is delivered. Isn't that what we see so uncannily paired together in Job's strange answer, "The Lord gives and the Lord takes away. Blessed be the name of the Lord"?

The recipient of a message must be prepared even before he opens the message for either the blow that comes with bad news or the joy that comes with good. In the Book of Joshua we are told the story of a divine messenger whose duty it was to tell the Hebrews that they would suffer a severe setback in occupying the Promised Land. His message moved the people to tears. Indeed, they were so deeply moved by the message that henceforth they called the place where they received it *"Bokim"* (weeping). So then, just as we experience moments of joy and sorrow in opening human messages, so we experience joy and sorrow at messages from God.

The people we call prophets were nothing less than messengers from God. They had the same function as angels. In those days an entire era was characterized by a message of misfortune to come. It was not by coincidence that in those days God announced the coming of judgment through a human agent. Obviously it was necessary for God to send messengers so that people would understand his will.

Are There Really Angels?

No! There are no angels. Even in the Bible there is nothing of the kind. The Bible frequently reports—and quite matter-of-factly at that—that a messenger or angel of God came to someone and did this or said that. But that is quite another matter. The question of whether there are angels is a red herring that we simply must avoid, for angels have no existence, no being in a sense comparable to what we mean when we speak of human existence. For example, the question "Is there a God?" has as little to do with the reality of God as the question "Are there really angels?" The old Scholastic philosophers and theologians answered the question about the existence of God by calling him the highest form of existence. But even this answer sought to fit God into our human concept of being, and rather naively at that. The question of God's reality simply cannot be answered in this way.

From a purely objective point of view, angels are as inaccessible as God himself. The matter of the being or existence of angels cannot be established. The Bible never speaks of the being or existence of angels per se. It does, however, report the comings of messengers of God. But only the one to whom such a messenger of God comes can testify to that. What is passed down to us about angels is always only the point of contact, the moment of encounter, a word or a deed. It is precisely in the encounter, the word or deed, that a messenger of God shows himself to be such, but at the same time he defies all our attempts to nail him down, understand him, fit him into our categories of thought and perception. We just cannot lay hold of angels in any way—either intellectually or by imagination. In the old Bible stories about messengers of God it is clear that the one to whom the messenger comes recognizes him as a messenger of God only after his departure. It is not the messenger's form or appearance, or what makes him tangible or recognizable, that makes him a messenger of God, but rather his message and his message alone.

Are there really angels? That is not the question to ask about a messenger of God. Instead, we need to ask, Does God send messengers to us here on earth? The answer to that is an emphatic yes! Throughout the Bible, witness to that is borne by those to whom the messengers came.

The Announcement

Our entire existence is played off between routine, everyday events, the memory of which we bury in our subconscious, and special events and moments that are long remembered. These special events and moments do not necessarily have to cast their shadows before them, but frequently they do just that. The beginning of Franz Werfel's novel *The Forty Days of Musa Dagh* is an excellent example of how coming events cast their shadow before them. It seems to be peculiarly characteristic of human existence that special events have about them a dimension which goes beyond our concept of time. These events are not there only in that moment in which they take place; in some inexplicable way they are there beforehand. This can be said of an individual's life as well as of the life of a group.

Behind this idea is the feeling that the events in our lives, particularly the significant events, come from far off, that they are something different from chemical or physical processes. It is this premonition of this other dimension which may be behind much of today's interest in astrology, for astrology, too, works on the supposition that what happens in our lives is fixed in advance in a somewhere beyond us, and that a human being can have some foreknowledge of what is coming before it happens. In the main the supposition is the same. The astounding thing is that the very people who cannot identify that other dimension of events with a personal and living God see their fate anchored in the position of the stars and wait to see in the stars the announcement of what to expect in the future.

However one may judge it, the flourishing of astrology in our day is a clear sign that we lack that of which we ought to be aware, particularly where our existence runs in many fixed channels. People wait for the message, an angel, and read their horoscopes. If they wait with great dedication, they will quickly note that a prediction can never take the place of an announcement.

There have always been all kinds of *predictions* and there will always be such predictions. The *announcement* of what *is to be* will remain the unusual and miraculous. It belongs to the nature of the announcement that, along with the words which announce what is coming, he who sent the message is also heard. An announcement therefore makes known in a human life something entirely different from what a prediction makes known. A prediction produces a certain tension from the moment it is heard until the moment that which is predicted either does or does not come to pass. If someone sets a great deal of store by such predictions and keeps trying to discover something about his future, then his life is like a fever chart—filled with ups and downs. If one trusts him from whom the announcement comes, then something else becomes of this tension. He who receives the message can confidently and patiently rely on what is announced to him. And when that which has been announced comes to pass, the memory of the announcement will linger and leave a lasting effect on him who heard it, and he will be bound to the one who sent the message. The life of one who has received a message can be likened to the line of a mountain range on the distant horizon, a line that rises from a level to a peak and then gradually slopes off to a level. We see this in the life of Mary, our Lord's mother, who in the course of a simple life received a message, experienced the fulfillment of what was announced, and then settled back into the routine of life.

Angels' Wings

When he was called to be a prophet, Isaiah saw the Lord high and lifted up. He also saw winged seraphim standing around the Lord. In many parts of the ancient world these winged creatures were portrayed as belonging to the court of God. They are not messengers of God, but they are in the message of the messenger. On the one hand, the messengers of God, and on the other, the heavenly creatures of God's court (the seraphim or cherubim, or the forces of nature that serve him) belong to two distinctly different circles of conception. The seraphim and cherubim do not depict two separate troops of a class of creatures that are broadly called angels. That idea came later, when the concept of angels became the predominant concept to which the several kinds of lesser angels then became subordinate. And thus it happened that from Isaiah's description of the winged cherubim and seraphim all angels were thought of as having wings.

In a sense, wings have become a kind of uniform for angels, and this development is noteworthy in itself.

Over the years human thought has shown a strong tendency to move toward general concepts. Where an idea moved further from us—that is, beyond human ability to contain it—people could master it only by subordinating it to some general concept. This inclusion in a general concept is in fact similar to clothing the idea in a uniform. We need only recall the times in which this garbing in uniform prevailed in order to see what kind of general effect it had. The human mind dressed angels in a uniform of wings, but that mentality no longer understood the uniform because angels no longer confronted man. God's messenger does not need wings.

The winged cherubim and seraphim—mostly in the shape of such animals as lions—go back thousands of years. We find them in a large number of pictures that have come down to us from antiquity. Where they are depicted on temple walls, ritual vessels, or the thrones or statues of deities, they point to the nearness of deity. It is quite likely that when Isaiah had his vision of God upon his throne he also had in mind the cherubim portrayed on the walls of Jerusalem. It would not be out of place in our day to associate these winged creatures with technology. There is a connection between the end of the mythical depiction of the world and the goal-conscious endeavor—which is difficult to understand—with which a humankind come of age builds its own wings. When flying creatures ceased to be the necessary marks of the divine sphere, flying became incorporated into the realm of human possibilities. One cannot just flatly say that something was taken away from the divine sphere. One has to admit that the relationship between a humankind now capable of flying and the sphere of divinity is fundamentally different from that in mythical thought. One would have to risk the next step and incorporate this new possibility of flying into our relationship to God in our time. In a recently published listing of the world's most dangerous professions, jet test pilots took first place. That has something to say to us.

A few years ago the newspapers were filled with reports of a plane crash over the Nevada desert. Two large passenger planes had collided during a storm, and more than a hundred passengers lost their lives. This new kind of catastrophe speaks its own language. The new possibility that flying gives to humankind would not be so gripping if it did not also include a new possibility of sudden death. It is more fitting for a pilot or a passenger to commend himself to God's care at the moment of takeoff than it is for a farmer to do so when climbing up on his tractor.

The seraphim's wings that Isaiah saw in his vision are not for the purpose of transporting the messenger. As I have said, the seraphim are not messengers. The seraphim have the appearance of animals, just as do many Egyptian deities, as a reminder of that distant mythical world in which man stood in a relationship between the divine and animal powers which we no longer understand.

In our world the works of humans, namely, machines

and technology, take the place of the mythical, animal-like powers. This kind of power cannot, however, make God smaller or less. He can incorporate them into his acting just as he once—in the beginning—conquered the mythical powers and made them his servants.

The White Garb

One of the most noteworthy things about angels is that they are usually dressed in white. An angel is often one whose raiment is "white as snow" (Matt. 28:3). Do angels really need clothes? When the question is asked as coarsely as this, we must say, No, an angel does not wear clothes; an angel is garbed or attired. When we think of garb or attire we usually think of formal dress, the rather old-fashioned attire we wear to very formal affairs. Angels do not wear sport jackets. But why not? Do we really think angels wear clothes or garb or attire because they need to? They are clothed—or if you prefer, garbed or attired—solely for the sake of those who encounter them. It is solely for their sake that angels are dressed in an inconspicuous way. There are stories of angels which make the point that the ones to whom the angels come do not recognize them. That is possible only if an angel is not recognizable by his dress. Today it would be difficult for an angel to conceal his identity if he were wearing formal or old-fashioned dress. If we dare to think of the possibility of angels encountering us today—

I don't mean fantasy figures, I mean messengers of whom the Bible speaks—then they must be garbed in modern dress.

All this means that there is a difference. The Bible also speaks of angels who are recognized immediately as such. Such angels "appear"; the others simply "come." Angelic garb is as varied as one angel's mission is different from another's. The garb is suited to the angel's function.

Our inquiry about the wearing apparel of angels is inseparable from inquiry about our own clothing. As we pursue the subject we find such a variety and changeableness of the meaning of clothing that a simple answer is impossible. Clothing can mean concealment, decoration, or protection, for example, from the cold. The many kinds of clothing and the many-sided meanings show that clothing is peculiar to human beings. At this point let me remind the reader of a strange contradiction that is characteristic of our clothing today. In addition to trying to stand out by wearing the nicest clothes, we try equally hard to choose the kind of clothing that is not conspicuous. On the one hand, then, clothing has a decorative function, on the other, a concealing one.

I said before that formal attire was not appropriate for angels. The Bible makes this clearer. The seraphim and cherubim that Isaiah saw around God's throne, and the cherubim at the gate of the Garden of Eden, were not clothed at all. Isaiah very clearly says "with two [wings] he covered his face . . . feet" (Isa. 6:2). We know something of what these cherubim looked like because we are in possession of many portrayals recovered from the past.

Clothing belongs to the messenger of God because it portrays that messenger in human form. He is clothed because he encounters people in their own territory, and the function of the clothing is not decorative but camouflaging. The messengers of God who came to Abraham or Gideon or the parents of Samson were dressed quite unostentatiously. Now, if we are serious in asking what the Bible means by a messenger of God, we must discard our customary ideas about angels and accept the fact that we just cannot pictorialize them. Then we must go a step beyond and admit that angels cannot even be imagined. The garb of angels belongs to the mystery of the messenger of God. Such a messenger can come in any kind of dress. We can never say, "An angel can't look like that." Clothing is a part of an angel because it enables him to come unostentatiously and yet in a way that is in keeping with the times.

It is not easy for us to give up our traditional ideas about angels; after all, we have had these ideas for a long time. But if we insist on holding on to the traditional garb of angels, we will not be able to grasp the truth that God sends messengers. The garb of angels is part and parcel of their being sent to humankind. An angel comes so close to humans that his closeness demands clothing just like that of human beings. Whether that is festive clothing—white, for example—that points from afar to God's glory, or inconspicuous, everyday clothing that makes him unrecognizable as a messenger of God, both kinds of clothing are a kind of concealment. The garb or attire of an angel is part of his not being able to be grasped by the minds of men and women. No one has ever seen an angel per se. What has been seen are only messengers, who themselves were hidden.

The Guardian Angel

On the dashboards of many a wrecked automobile we often see all kinds of mascots and good-luck charms. Sometimes these mascots are in the form of animals or dolls or even baby shoes. In a real sense these mascots are the modern descendants of guardian angels. Mascots and guardian angels share something very basic: they are an unmistakable sign of an inner, spiritual emptiness. Everyone—believer and nonbeliever alike—knows that we must look for protection not to a mascot but to another. Every such mascot is a splinter of a faith that has been lost. It is also a sign that can compel us to lament that today's person—precisely at the point where it is a matter of security, protection, and preservation of life—sinks back into the past to lay hold of and bring to the surface a remnant of one's animistic past. What a bizarre picture this presents: automobiles, motorcycles, trucks, airplanes—all so representative of the technological advances of our day—and people carry talismans, the marks of human mentality sinking back into extreme primitiveness.

The idea of a guardian angel marks a considerable advance of the human spirit over against talismans, charms, and the like. In fact, the idea of a guardian angel, though laughable to some, is a much more modern and advanced idea than the charms and talismans that people carry around in their automobiles. Perhaps I can make this matter clearer on the basis of my initial example. If someone attributes a kind of protecting power to some object (even though this may be done only in jest), one is attributing the power to help (again, perhaps only in jest) to something which itself inevitably comes to destruction, for example, an automobile or its occupants. Such a thing was entirely possible for primitive people because they could not imagine such a possibility. But people in our confused day and age can attribute a power to protect to talismans because people to a great extent have lost the power to think in terms of cause, effect, and relationship.

Belief in guardian angels took the idea of protecting, preserving, and watching out of the sphere of that which itself can be destroyed. A guardian angel is far more than a talisman or a charm, for an angel can never be caught up in catastrophes. One can keep his faith in guardian angels in spite of catastrophes. A guardian angel, to be sure, is as much a guarantee against accidents as are talismans. But a guardian angel is closer to the enigmatic unfathomability of a misfortune that has befallen one than is a talisman.

I often have the feeling that these automobile charms and talismans, as well as other such objects that are taken more seriously, could be something more than just reminders of a faith that has been lost. They could quite well be the outstretching of hands of those who can no longer pray.

It really does not matter much whether one believes in a guardian angel as one goes about the routines of life. What does matter, however, is that when one goes through the "valley of the shadow," one does so in the sure and certain knowledge that "thou art with me." The person who knows this detects the angel in God's help. To see God's angel means here nothing else but to experience being saved from the very brink of death, as a part of the story of God's dealing with me. The angel, then, is quite simply God's help which is near at hand to me. All our thinking, understanding, and mental images can recede completely in speaking of and trusting in and experiencing a guardian angel whom God sends to me when I am in danger.

The Seaman's Angel

In southern France close to the Spanish border on the Atlantic Coast, where the Bay of Biscay beats against the cliffs, there is a church. It is a small church, a comparatively new edifice that was built for the seamen who live in the vicinity. Upon entering the church one's eye is immediately caught by a picture that occupies the entire chancel area. The painting depicts Christ walking across the waves toward a storm-tossed ship.

I stood for a long time before that painting because it spoke a powerful language. I knew it must have a powerful impact upon the seamen who entered this church, and their wives and children as well. For them this picture is true to life. In the face of this reality the question whether the story in the Gospels is true simply pales.

When I saw that picture I wanted to be one of those seamen who saw their reality in the picture. And yet at the same time I knew that in my own situation I was one of those who could no longer believe the story of Christ's walking on the water. Today I keep asking myself if we can recover this Gospel story only by openly and unreservedly accepting its legendary character. That would mean that a later motif has been retrojected upon Jesus of Nazareth, a motif that is nothing else but the motif of the guardian, saving angel who comes to the aid of those endangered by that storm. This motif, which is found in the many stories that are told wherever sailors get together, is made of the real, solid stuff of experience. It has about it the ring of reality. Such stories have been told by many who were saved. Ps. 107:23–32 is just such an account.

It comes naturally to us to think of some incident involving the sea when we are looking for an example of a "rescue." The basics of this kind of rescue correspond to the basics of the need. The less a human possibility of rescue is involved, the more certain one is of having been helped and rescued by one who is earnestly invoked, the mighty One who comes from beyond. The mental images we use to express the help we received, the experience of being rescued, are of secondary, if indeed of any, importance.

As humankind learned to tame the elements, and as the number of people who were forced to struggle with the raw elements of nature for daily survival diminished, the further the certain experience of having been rescued receded, and the less this experience could be representative of a class of people. It is then that the attempt to preserve the mental image of an experience which lies in the distant past becomes an illusion. We can no longer see the situation as did the fishermen, for whom the experience was a real-life situation. Something else is more important, namely, that the experiences of being rescued are still renewed and preserved for our world. People still tell of having been rescued in such remarkable ways that the rescuer can be spoken of only as one who comes from "another place," who comes from the shore to that place where one is helplessly tossed about. The guardian angel can come only where the need is great. But one does not have to believe in angels where the waves surge and the storm rages; the angels come to one who is saved. Later on, when one tells of what has happened and perceives what has happened as a case of "having made it again," then no one has encountered him at all. The fact that one was saved is testimony to one's having been encountered. The word *rescue* can never be separated from the rescuer. And beyond every rescuer stands the one who is the Lord of all. Rescue from raw, elemental forces is something that we experience in our day and age only when our work compels us to face these forces. We encounter these raw forces naked, alone, and unarmed only in exceptional instances. It would be idle romanticism to think otherwise.

My thoughts keep returning to the chancel painting in that little church. The rescue it depicts is that of an individual struggling against the raw elements. People who are threatened and tossed about by the waves and subjected to the raging of the storm are not rescued by walking on the waves. Rather, they experience the rescue in the rescued ship; they are rescued along with something they made with their own hands.

We forget all too easily what a gigantic step of technological progress that ship represented. But then, don't we call airplanes "ships"? So the work of human hands is woven into the story of the rescue. Here we have the presupposition that the collision of a human being with the raw forces of nature is more violent and intense where the person is armed. It is here that we get a glimpse of a new step of technological existence, a step that puts us in a position to combine the triumph and intoxication of new airships and new motion as well as those of needs, catastrophes, and rescues of a person who is powerfully armed with a new faith against raw forces. In that new faith the new ships have their new angels, and those who are rescued tell of him who came to them over the waves.

The Angel with a
Flaming Sword

The garden from which Adam and Eve were expelled because of their sin of disobedience is guarded by an angel with a flaming sword. There are certain areas in life that can be guarded only by "the other side." There are and always will be areas of life that humankind just cannot reach for so long as humans exist. Mortals can take various positions on this. They can act as though that other side did not exist, and they can even go to great ends to prove that there can be no other side. On the other hand, they can expend considerable mental and even physical energy in the attempt to turn what they acknowledge to be the other side into "this" side.

All these attempts are ridiculous in view of the angel with the flaming sword. Against this angel one can accomplish very little, for fighting him is like tilting against a windmill. This angel stands watch over the realm of God, where one can lay eyes on God without dying. To behold the deity is forbidden to mortal men and women.

It is at this boundary point between the divine and the

human that the angel with the flaming sword stands guard. Here many may stop short or react with horror. An angel with a sword? Angels with swords are encountered elsewhere in the Bible, but in entirely different contexts. The Bible does not hesitate in the least to put a sword in the hand of an angel, whom we usually think of as holding a harp. Indeed, it can be necessary for an angel to wield a sword. The sword symbolizes the authority to inflict the penalty of death, and a nobility is conferred upon this sword so that authority will not perish. No human power can negate this nobility. Romans 13 speaks of the office of the sword and calls it "God's servant." The angels are God's servants in a proper sense. In the Bible, serving is a personal, two-sided matter. When a government has broken off every relationship to God, it can no longer be a servant of God. What God is to the state in a world that has become quite religionless is perhaps best suggested by the term "toleration of churches and religious fellowships." Such toleration, intentionally or not, is a kind of recognition of God. But if it is understood to be a toleration based on the premise that "as long as the churches have not entirely closed down, we will tolerate them," then that toleration is no longer a recognition of God. Such a government cannot be a servant of God. It is sheer madness to assert that a government is a servant of God simply because it is a government.

If these were the only kind of governments on earth, the sword—the power of a government to inflict death—would have lost its noble character, and these governments would of necessity have to perish. Why must there be some kind of judicial authority and power among mortals? Why does the Bible put the sword into the hands of an angel, the real servant of God? If our answer were that human beings are evil and that there must be an authority appointed by God which has the power and right to inflict the penalty of death, then we would face a dilemma. A watchman does not stand guard over a city because it is full of condemned people. Even if the angel's flaming sword made the realm of God completely inaccessible, that sword nonetheless remains the weapon of an individual engaged in battle against many individuals. God does not post heavenly legions at the entrance to the garden; he posts just one angel with a sword.

Perhaps over the past two thousand years the church has generalized the idea of human depravity to an extent that we today can no longer do. We can no longer generalize this idea because the masses of the twentieth century have lost their ability to be evil. Somehow today it is no longer important whether or not all people are evil. What is more important is the concentration of evil in the individual. The angel with the flaming sword can never be confronted by the masses. The masses can never confront anything. Moreover, the angel with the flaming sword can do nothing against the masses. He stands where he stands, against individuals and, under certain circumstances, against groups; in other words, he stands only against those who are capable of evil.

The extermination of masses of people through

sophisticated weaponry and all manner of destructive force no longer has anything to do with the sword. But it is precisely such weapons that demonstrate the original intent of the sword. The angel has the flaming sword in order to keep mortals at a distance from God's own realm. It also prevents people from manipulating and mastering death as though they were God. The sword is there for those who give the order and for those who, with a push of the button, unleash the force of deadly weapons. Anyone who gives a thought to the angel with the flaming sword who is posted at the entrance of God's garden cannot lose confidence, not even in the face of the possibility of the annihilation that humans now have at their disposal. Nor will one be able to say that anyone stands powerless over against them. Anyone who gives a thought to that angel with the flaming sword knows that however great and powerful one's power to destroy may be, an indestructible realm still remains. The garden before which God's angel is posted is, according to the old story, here on this earth—even though it is the realm of God.

That garden was and still is intended for us, in spite of the angel with the flaming sword. The angel stands watch there to preserve that garden for humankind. Because this angel is there, mortal humans, however extreme their affliction may be, can maintain the sense of nobility and worth that no torturing, disquieting power can take from them.

Music-making Angels

As I write I have in mind a painting by Mathias Gruenewald. Indeed, the thought of this picture reminds me of
a great many other pictures of angels singing and playing
a variety of instruments. Some depict just one such
angel, others two, and still others whole choirs of angels.

One can only marvel at the simplicity of these pictures, which not only put contemporary instruments
into the hands of angels but even portray them as
reading music. Quite honestly, one must admit that in
pictures of this kind the artists portray the playing of
music in ways with which they were familiar, and the
only purpose these angels serve is to elevate this music to
a higher sphere.

If we bear this in mind, then those music-making
angels of the Middle Ages still have the power to say
something that has meaning for our day and age. They
say that our inclusion of music in the ranks of the arts is
lacking, indeed, that it can conceal something very
essential. Music-making angels tell us that music has a
unique relationship to the praise of God. This praise of

God can never be integrated into our concept of art because the praise of God is a act that embraces all creation. Human voices raised in song are closer to the nonhuman creation than speaking voices, and the voices of instruments place human music-making in a much broader choir that embraces the inanimate creation. Seen in this light, the music-making of the angels takes on a deep and authentic meaning that is communicated with particular clarity by Gruenewald's painting.

The Angel and the Ass

In the Old Testament (Numbers 22–24) we find the story of a prophet who is ordered by a king at war with Israel to put a curse on the Israelite army. But God has the prophet pronounce a blessing instead of a curse. Early in the morning Balaam the prophet mounts his ass and rides to King Balak, who had summoned him. "But . . . the angel of the Lord took his stand in the way as his adversary . . . with a drawn sword in his hand." Sensing the presence of the angel coming toward them, the ass turned off the road. Balaam, who sensed nothing, struck the poor beast. The same thing occurred twice more. When Balaam struck the poor animal a third time, it opened its mouth and said, "What have I done to you, that you have struck me these three times?" Balaam, as though it were the most natural thing in the world for an animal to speak to him, answered the beast. It was not until the end of the conversation that Balaam's eyes were opened and he realized that the Lord's angel was standing in the way with a drawn sword in his hand.

Finally the prophet does what his animal had done: he bows before the angel.

The point of the story is that the ass was able to sense the confrontation by God's messenger better than a human being. The animal sensed the approach of the angel and got out of his way. But the human, the prophet, was dense, blind, totally unaware of the angel. Even though the prophet was a man of God, his eyes had to be opened so that he could become aware of the angel's presence. If the animal had not turned aside, the angel's sword would have struck. Balaam had the animal to thank that he survived the confrontation.

If we look at this story not as enlightened modern men and women who know better about everything, but rather with a readiness to listen, then we will hear something in it that would do our world good to hear. Our mechanized world has little appreciation for animals; we push them to the periphery of our thoughts. But they are creatures, and as such they share in our humanity. We cannot deny them their share without consequence. There is always a point at which animals have a better and sharper alertness than do people. There are moments when it is right and good for people to learn from and heed animals.

The ability to meet that "something other" that confronts humans is what this story is about. The animals, which are also living creatures, have kept their relationship to the Creator even though that relationship is concealed and closed to us. The Bible intimates this repeatedly. Even today a human being can be led through an animal out of blindness and insensitivity to that which confronts us from beyond.

Lovely as an Angel

Astonishing as it may seem to many, beauty queens do not make the world more beautiful. For us the idea of loveliness is inseparably bound up with the extent and degree of loveliness. That a lovely person—man or woman—excels in loveliness, is lovelier than, or is the loveliest is something people will perceive and discuss until the end of time. These points are so emphasized and exaggerated in the beauty contests of our day that such contests have become more a sign of impoverishment than a heaping of beauty.

But we must recognize that in today's beauty contests, indeed, in everything that is lovely—above all, everyone who is lovely—something tugs our hearts toward a loveliness that is transcendental. This is why people do not say that something or someone is as lovely as this or that actress or beauty queen. Rather, they say "lovely as an angel."

But how in the world do we know that angels are lovely? If we were to think of the pictures of angels we have seen, we certainly would not use the expression anymore. The comparison really has nothing to do with pictures of angels. One has instead the feeling that those feeble efforts to paint pictures of the loveliness of angels are simply weak reflections of a certainty people have that angels must be lovely. There is, however, no evidence for this. Whether the angel who came to Gideon was a lovely person or not is not important. He was there for the sake of the message he had to give, not to impress Gideon with his loveliness.

Actually it is probably the other way around. Angels must be lovely because all that is beautiful and lovely has something angelic about it. And all loveliness has about it something of a message. Genuine beauty and loveliness come from "beyond." This truth can be forgotten all too easily by someone who wants to measure and standardize beauty and loveliness. There is entirely too much of that today, but perhaps it just cannot be avoided in a day and age that wants to define, categorize, and make everything uniform. For a film star—if one is really lovely—to typify loveliness is not at all bad; it indicates the effect that the power of loveliness has on us.

At the same time, it is not good when loveliness becomes a worn-out expression. And here we observe something unusual. Because it is impossible to paint with oil the beauty of angels, angels are portrayed as doll-like—stereotyped and absurd. Today we see something similar happening with the faces of women! It is all a sign of our poverty, yet at the same time it is a sign of our yearning for that which is beautiful and lovely in the genuine sense of the words. Be all that as it may, loveliness will continue to assert itself, for loveliness comes to us just as angels come. And because this is so, even an ugly face can be lovely. The shining forth of the lovely in an ugly or uninteresting face does more to keep loveliness alive than does a bevy of beauty queens.

Because loveliness is something that confronts us, it always has about it something of the incomprehensibility of angels. The fact is that angels can be grasped in human terms as little as we can measure or stereotype or otherwise nail down the loveliness that encounters us in human form. This loveliness confronts us, that is, it comes and goes. Nothing can compel loveliness, and nothing can lay hold of it. Loveliness would not be loveliness if it did not come from the unknown and from our perception of its coming and going. Indeed, lovely as an angel!

The Joy of the Angels

"I tell you, there is joy before the angels of God over one
sinner who repents."

—Luke 15:10

In this saying of Jesus we find the secret of repentance.
This repentance is an event that cannot find its fitting
echo among humankind. People will misunderstand,
exaggerate, or exploit it. But the fact of the matter is that
repentance finds its only fitting echo in the joy of God
and the angels.

It is truly a wonderful thing when a person admits
having gone the wrong way in life and strikes out on a
new path. This admission does not come easily for
anyone. If the admission is genuine and not just pretense
or sham, it awakens shame in everyone. If one is not
ashamed to admit having gone the wrong way, then
one's repentance is not worth much. This is why it is
quite in order for someone who has repented to be
reluctant to speak about it. Repentance can also be a
shameless act. This is the case where repentance is
stretched out as well as where, in retrospect, repentance

is shamelessly sidestepped. This has to be said in order to preserve the dignity of repentance. Under the current terms of repentance—penance, confession, admission of sin—we can no longer recognize in its original sense the opportunity given by God to make a break with a misspent past and to strike out in a new direction.

This striking out in a new direction is one of humankind's highest and most significant abilities. That can be recognized, for example, where one is tempted to make this power of repentance, the admission of having gone the wrong way and the promise to strike out in a new direction, subservient to a political system. The politicization of repentance is a horrifying sign of our time. It is only in the joy of angels that the repentance of a single individual among us finds its proper and fitting echo. That is why repentance is worthwhile and, mindful of the joy of the angels, the one who repents no longer needs to be ashamed.

An Angel Comes from Another World: The Angel of Death

There is a saying among certain African tribesmen to the effect that an old man comes from "another world." There is something to this piece of popular wisdom. The pastor who officiated at the funeral of my father quoted this saying. I remember well the thought that came into my mind at that time. I was thinking of a certain moment in my life. There was a pathway leading through a forest of young but high pine trees—a straight, narrow way, really not much more than a footpath. Even in the hot summer that forest was cool, shady, and fragrant. On this pathway I saw the bent figure of my father, hobbling along on a cane, his white hair bright against the shade of the forest. I entertained a thought somewhat similar to this African saying. I thought that quite often an old person has a message from another world, a message from far, far away. The thought was not one that I could summarize in a single sentence, but at that moment I could sense that there must be some meaning in a person's growing old and tired and feeble, indeed, in everything moving close to death. There is something good and beautiful and awe-inspiring in that. I felt as though I had to fall on my knees in reverence.

Death is one of those events in life that can be announced to a person. Every people has its ancient stories that say or illustrate this in one way or another. Among Germans, some of the old fairy tales hold that Death is its own messenger, who comes to a person who is soon to die. Death, to which all that lives and breathes must come, affords the most compelling example of how events in life can be such that they announce themselves in an endless multiplicity of ways.

It is not a message when a person senses that his end is near. A message is there only when something like an announcement is heard, something like a call across the great divide. The mere apprehension of impending death has both possibilities. Such an apprehension can be like the undertow of an abyss which draws one into this apprehension. It can also be a word to which I can entrust myself. Therein lies the reality of the angel of death. The one whom I can trust is the one who says to me that my hour has come. The angel of death is the one who makes me aware that death is one of God's possibilities with me.

Part Two

Two Messages of Salvation

In what the Old Testament has to say about angels we can discern three time periods. Here and there in the narrative writings of the earliest of the three periods, angels are mentioned quite matter-of-factly. What is said is never in detail, and one cannot sense any special interest in angels. They were simply accepted as part of the reality of the time, as were God, nature, and animals. In the second period, that of the preexilic prophets, Deuteronomy, and the priestly writing (included in the framework of the five books of Moses, which took shape in priestly circles toward the end of the Babylonian exile or shortly thereafter), nothing—or at least as good as nothing—is said about angels. Around the end of the Babylonian exile, however, we notice an interest in angels which begins with Ezekiel. This interest is considerably intensified with Zechariah, and it leads to the developed doctrine of angels which turns up in the apocalyptic literature. This doctrine is set forth in detail in the apocryphal books (e.g., Enoch) and is taken for granted by the Book of Daniel, which dates back to 165–164 B.C.

In the first of these three periods we do not have a matter of angels in general but "the angels of God." It seems clear that in these three periods angels are spoken of in a variety of ways, and one must be cautious about making any kind of generalization.

In the early stories about the angels of God, one line of thought is particularly important, namely, that an angel is not actually a form alongside of or somewhat lower than God himself, but is rather God's word or act touching the earth. In one and the same story the narrator can speak of God appearing instead of an angel, and of an angel appearing in place of God, as a way of expressing God's word touching the earth. Quite often the angel of God who comes to human beings does so as another person, as a traveler who comes to them to make something known. In the first of the three periods the angel stories all deal with this messenger of God. Then, too, there is talk about an angel who accompanies and protects, and often about an angel who brings some kind of ruination; for example, an angel accompanied the Hebrews in the wilderness (see Exod. 14:19).

There are only two major themes that recur in the stories telling of the message of an angel. These themes are the two situations of need to which God's messenger brings a message of deliverance: the primal need of man and the primal need of woman. For the woman the message is that she is to bear a child; for the man the message is that he shall be delivered from oppression.

It is no coincidence that we encounter angelic announcements of impending births in the stories of the patriarchs and announcements of deliverance at early points of Hebrew national history. The birth of a child is the major theme of the patriarchal stories. The announcement through a messenger of God of the impending birth of a child has a special place in the Abraham stories. In Genesis 16 the birth of Ishmael is announced to Hagar. It is one of the loveliest stories in the Bible, and it tells about God's angel coming to Hagar, the concubine of Abraham. She was harassed and finally driven out by her mistress, Sarah, and then was encountered in her sore distress in the wilderness by an angel, the messenger of God. This angel asked her where she came from and where she was going. Then the angel sent her back to her mistress, not empty-handed, but with a promise with which Hagar could live, namely, the promise that she would bear a child who would become the father of a great nation. This story makes it particularly clear that it is not possible to make a sharp distinction between God and his messenger in these early stories. After the angel departed from her, Hagar said, "Have I really seen God and remained alive after seeing him?"

Let us compare two announcements of a birth.

Gen. 16.8ff.	*Luke 1:28ff.*
V.8: Angelic salutation.	V.28: Angelic salutation.
V.11: "Behold, you are with child, and shall bear a son; you shall call his name Ishmael; because the Lord has given heed to your affliction."	V.31: "And behold, you will conceive in your womb and bear a son, and you shall call his name Jesus."
	V.30: "You have found favor with God."
V.12: "He shall be. . . ."	V.32: "He will be great. . . ."

There are a number of similar stories, for example, the parallel to Hagar's encounter with an angel found in Genesis 21. Here, after she had given birth to her child, the two of them almost perish from thirst. It is then that the angel calls down from heaven the word of promise. Here the promise is bound up with deliverance from death by thirst instead of with announcement of the birth of a child.

The other and more important birth of a child found in the Abraham stories deals with the birth of Isaac, which is also announced by a messenger of God in Genesis 18's account of the three men who sojourn with Abraham. Here the announcement is mainly directed to the father-to-be. Here, too, a parallel to Luke 1 is seen. While the announcement of Jesus' birth is made to the mother, that of the birth of John the Baptist is announced to the father. And in all four cases mentioned here, the announcement is made by a messenger. In the Old as well as in the New Testament the story of deliverance begins with the announcement of the birth of a child. A child must be born so that God can do his work among humankind.

The announcement of the birth of a child occurs at other points in the Bible. A messenger of God announced the birth of a child to the parents of Samson (Judges 13). In the story of Hannah, the mother of Samuel, it is a priest rather than an angel who made the announcement (1 Samuel 1). Elisha the prophet announced to the Shunammite woman that within a year she would hold a child to her breast (2 Kings 4).

The cycle of these stories, which are alike in so many ways, permits us to conclude that there probably was an ancient way of portraying such an event which lent itself to the formation of the story as it had been shaped by others hundreds of years before. The power of such a pattern is to be found in the event which remained the same through the ages. In a society in which women found fulfillment, honor, recognition, and happiness solely by bearing children, the worst thing that could happen to a woman was to be childless. To give birth to a child, then, was the most specific and uniquely female experience of deliverance. Over the course of the centuries this experience has found an echo we can understand in a story form in which an angel plays the major role. What are we to make of that?

The experience of deliverance, which changed the life of the childless woman from one of misery to one of happiness, happened not at the moment when she realized she was pregnant or when she gave birth to the child but at the time the pregnancy and birth were first announced. This is why the angel who announces what is to come belongs to these stories. These women experienced their deliverance through a word that was spoken to them.

The stories that deal with the announcement to a woman of the impending birth of a child probably belong to the oldest portrayals of something akin to revelation to humankind. Such stories are the stories of revelation to women, and that revelation is directed to the special need of women. It is worth noting that the stories in which the transformation of this need of women is expressed center not on the birth of a child but on the announcement that a birth is to take place. The man's peculiar experience of deliverance, which has its center in a verbal event, is an unmistakable sign of this. The deliverance comes through the annunciatory word of the messenger, and the experiences of deliverance comes with the hearing and acceptance of this word. When the mothers, whose lives had been so wonderfully transformed, later told others about this turning point in their time of need, the high point of their recital was the coming of the messenger. This is something that runs throughout the Bible.

The transformation of the need of the people—that is, the specific need of men—is transmitted in the same way throughout the Bible. For them, the turning point is the announcement of the deliverance to come. We see this in the case of the Hebrews in bondage in Egypt. Even the gospel—the good news—derives its name from this announcement of deliverance. Deliverance comes as the announcement of good news. The focal point is that moment in which the good news is announced and accepted.

To this experience of deliverance belong those stories announcing the birth of a child as well as those that announce deliverance from a threatening danger. These two groups of stories are joined by the angel, the messenger of God, who is prominent in both. Behind all this is a God who performs his saving acts for humankind by coming to people in his word. Seen in this light, both groups of angel stories have significance for the entire Bible and for our faith as well.

The announcement of deliverance from threatening danger by a messenger of God is seen in a beautiful way in the story of the calling of Gideon (Judges 6). In this story from the early history of the Hebrew people, we are told of a farmer's son at work threshing grain, not on the threshing floor but in a winepress that had been hewn out of a narrow depression in the vineyard. He threshed grain there because it was too dangerous to do it out in the open on the threshing floor. You see, the land was under the heel of a conqueror, and had the grain been threshed in the open, occupation troops could—and most likely would—simply confiscate it.

A messenger of God came to Gideon while he was threshing. The messenger was not recognizable as such; in fact, he looked like an ordinary human being. He greeted young Gideon with, "The Lord is with you, you mighty man of valor." Gideon took the greeting literally. (There was a time when greetings were taken literally.) Gideon replied in effect, "What does that mean, 'The Lord is with you?' I don't see him. Where are all those mighty deeds he used to do for his people?" The messenger then said that Gideon was destined to be the one through whom those great deeds would begin once again. Quite seriously the young man objected that he was not qualified. Whereupon the messenger answered that it was precisely through Gideon's helplessness that God would accomplish what he intended. Young Gideon listened, yet remained skeptical.

He wanted to know who would verify all this, for after all he did not know the angel. Furthermore, he countered, he was just an ordinary person, and the whole thing could be fraud.

At this point we reach the most astonishing part of the story. The messenger accepted the validity of Gideon's objections and gave him a sign to verify the message, a sign that Gideon could recognize. In the act of disappearing the visitor showed himself to be a messenger from the "other" world, and Gideon was able to recognize him for what he was. And what the messenger said would happen did indeed take place. Gideon, now certain that God had called him, gathered a band of men which drove the foe out of the land.

This story describes what a later age called inspiration. What the messenger said and did in the old stories was in later times attributed to man himself. The actual sending is looked upon as naïve, primitive, and legendary, and it is transformed into an awareness of being sent, whereby extraordinary deeds are explained as those of an inspired man. But this period in which one spoke of inspiration and of an awareness of being sent is only a transitional period. The idealism of every form can live only for a short while in the shadow of the genuine story of God. For a time God always permits himself to vanish into the cloud of an idea, and then all the faith words somehow become separated from God's deeds and become just so many empty words.

But as long as there are people on the face of the earth and they experience the zealousness of youth, there will be such a thing as inspiration. Moreover, there will always be people who know for certain that they are destined for some great thing. It really is not very important how people explain this phenomenon to themselves, nor is it of any importance that people—at least in their own minds—have become so clever and learned that they can dismiss as outdated the old stories of the coming of the messenger. But in preserving and listening to these stories, the relationship between dedication to a great deed and an awareness of the whole is preserved, maintained, and renewed. The bravery of what is dared, the deed that does not count the cost, originates in a world different from ours. We ourselves have no access to this other world, but a messenger comes from there to us.

Another story of the same stripe is the one in Joshua 5 about Joshua's confrontation with an angel. There we are told that when Joshua was at Jericho he raised his eyes and saw someone with a gleaming sword in his hand facing him. The sentence is similar to the one at the beginning of the story of Abraham's confrontation by angels. In Abraham's case, however, the messengers of God were sojourners. In Joshua's case it was a warrior that stood face-to-face with Joshua the warrior. One cannot tell, however, where that warrior came from. Joshua asked him whether he was friend or foe, and at that point the story breaks off. What the messenger of God had come to say is missing. We can only surmise that the messenger had come to announce to Joshua that the city of Jericho would fall to the Hebrews. Because just such a statement occurs in Josh. 6:2–3, it is likely that these verses belonged originally to the encounter with the angel.

The story of the burning bush (Exodus 3) is the first of a series of stories in which deliverance is announced to God's people through his messenger. Only once in this story of the calling of Moses does it say that it was a messenger of God who confronted Moses there. From there on it was always the Lord himself who spoke to Moses and who commissioned him. (Note that the story of Joshua's encounter with an angel contains—word for word—a sentence from Moses' call: the command to take off his shoes because the ground on which he stands is holy.)

In the story of the announcement of the impending birth of Samson, the two motifs of a message of a birth and a message of deliverance come together. Samson's mother was barren, childless. Not only was Samson's birth deliverance and joy for the mother, but to her was given the promise that her son would begin to rescue Israel from the hand of the Philistines. It is precisely here that we can see how one era flows into another. The angels who announced the impending birth of a child to Hagar, Sarah, and Abraham belong to a time when the family was the center of society. The family was the pre-state era of human history, a prehistoric era about which we know very little but which like bedrock thrusts itself into biblical accounts. The nomadic patriarchs represent this pre-state epoch in which the lords of the clans held sovereign sway. There was no clear line of division between the private and public spheres which is so important to us today. In those days a woman's childlessness was not a private matter overshadowed by the important events of public life but a crisis that put the whole of society in jeopardy.

We can scarcely imagine what it must have been like in those days when birth, marriage, conflict, harmony, and all the other familiar aspects of life were at one and the same time public and political matters. Nor can we imagine what it must have been like when the total economic life centered in the family, when the maintenance of the family, culture, religion, and custom were purely family matters. We can scarcely conceive of such a state of affairs in our day, and yet it seems very important that the era which was coming into being, in which emphasis came to be laid upon matters of state, embraced not the entire history of the world, but only one era after another. From then on the messenger of God brought a message concerning the deliverance of God's people from political need (the story of the birth of Samson shows this in transition). But even that did not remain so forever. The messages of God's messengers change.

Here there opens up a perspective that we dare not ignore. That earlier era, in which the messages of God's messengers consisted of announcements to barren women that they will bear a child, began to fade into the background, and the political era began.

With the coming of Christ a thoroughly nonpolitical message came to humankind at a time that was and still remains thoroughly political. But does that mean this must always be so? Can it not be that God's message, which came to earth in Jesus Christ and which was singularly intended for the entire earth, points toward an era yet to come, when the political element in human society will fade into the background, as did the familiar events at the dawning of the political era? Can we really be so certain from the Bible that church and state will always be in a state of essential polarization? I do not believe this to be the case. The Bible does not justify the conclusion that the political era of human history will endure until Christ comes again, that is, until the end of the world. In my opinion there are already many signs that the political structure of human relationships will not remain in its present form. It could be that in the changes in human relationships taking place in our day the church will miss out on something decisive. Above all, the church would have to ask if the form the church has taken over against that of the Western nations still corresponds to the actual intention of the message in the world.

In the collection of patriarchal stories, there are yet others that tell of encounters with angels which have nothing to do with the birth of a child or with deliverance in a political sense, but instead deal with preservation. The angels who had announced the birth of a son to Abraham (Genesis 18) returned to the house of Lot in Sodom. Here the messengers were cordially received, although Lot's hospitality was put sorely to the test. During the night, Lot and his family protected the angels against intruders who wanted to break into the house. The next morning the angels protected Lot from the catastrophe they had come to announce against Sodom. It is significant that—and it happens only here—the very angels who executed God's judgment upon the city also came to save one man and his family.

In the later version of the Hagar story (Genesis 21) we find not the announcement that a child will be born but the story of a child's preservation from death. Likewise, the story of Abraham's sacrifice in Genesis 22 is concerned with the preservation of a child, although that is not the chief motif. In the story of Jacob's dream at Bethel (Genesis 28), God told Jacob he was with him and would protect him wherever he went. To be sure, it was God himself who said this, but in the dream Jacob had he saw the angels of God going up and down a stairway that stretched up to heaven, and it was an angel who later told Jacob to return to his homeland.

In all these stories the angel of God, who comes as a messenger to men and women, acts very much like the guardian or guiding angel who is encountered in still other contexts and who cannot be sharply distinguished from God himself. The best example of a guiding angel in the patriarchal stories is the report of Isaac's betrothal to Rebekah in Genesis 24.

So, then, the encounters with angels in the patriarchal

stories all attest the message of deliverance to women in their primal need and the promise of guidance and preservation to men in their wanderings. In both types of story God's action touches the earth and draws near to mortals.

The Messengers of God

It is a peculiarity of the Bible that from beginning to end it speaks toward and into the future. The Bible has never been modern—if one understands "modern" to mean contemporary with us—because it was always much more interested in the future than in the present. For this reason the Bible can never be out-of-date. Man and his ways of life and living can change time and again, but the Bible is still far ahead of both. Entire sections and books of the Bible may be closed to our understanding for centuries. And then one day, in a changed world, their voices are heard to speak with astonishing clarity. Theologians have long attempted—and many still try—to understand the entire Bible at one time. That attempt ends and always will end in frustration. One attributes more to the Bible when one admits that there is much in the Bible that we cannot understand today. But the doors of understanding that are closed to us today can be opened to us tomorrow.

When I speak of angels in the Bible I do so not by looking backward but by looking forward. Angels as mythical beings, as half-divine, half-human figures with wings, special clothing, and doll-like faces, have ceased to exist for us. And such creatures are not what the Bible has in mind when it speaks of God's messengers, the angels. On the other hand, I have concluded from studying the Bible that these messengers of God cannot be eliminated, symbolized, spiritualized, or demythologized by some exegetical method or other without losing a major part of the Bible.

Without hesitation we should leave the whole business of the views and concepts of times past to the historians of religion, art, and literature. Such concepts belong to the past and, however piously we may conserve them, we will not change things in the least. The coming of one who is sent by God, the coming of the angel, belongs to the future. God will send his messengers. We do not know how.

I took a walk one evening some years ago through the streets of New York City. In a quiet, narrow street in the heart of the business district I saw rows of lighted windows that seemed to be cut out of the black heaven of night and rising out of a deep shaft to incomprehensible heights. In that moment something occurred to me that I would never have grasped in Europe, namely, that our concept of space has changed. "Above" and "below" do not mean for us what they meant for the people of ancient and medieval times. Today angels cannot appear as they once appeared to the shepherds at Christ's birth. They will come in other ways.

We do not know how the angels will come. And it

really does not matter whether we accept or reject the story of the appearance of angels to the shepherds as Luke 2 relates it. What does matter, however, is whether we believe that God sends his messengers. I should like to point out that such belief is possible only if we listen to the stories that the Bible reports. We exclude this possiblity when we make from what we read in the Bible our own mental picture of what angels are like or when we fabricate a doctrine about angels which we hold to be the only valid or correct doctrine. Actually, the Bible gives us no mental picture of angels, and it has no doctrine about them. If we listen to and compare the stories that report about angels, and if we either affirm or deny them, regard them as beautiful or doubt them, we will always make the significant observation that in the Bible angels are not at all religious. They almost never—or at least as good as never—confront us in the specifically religious contexts of worship, cultus, religious language, or theological reflection. The angels encountered Abraham in the noonday heat as he sat in the shade of his tent. They came to Gideon while he was threshing his father's grain. They came to Joshua as he was preparing for military action, to the shepherds as they kept watch over their flocks, and to a depressed woman in the privacy of her quarters. One could go on and on to show that throughout the entire Bible angels encounter men and women in the common places of life.

That means, then, that angels encounter people where, to our way of thinking, we would never expect to find messengers of God. In this respect we have a concept of angels which is contrary to that of the Bible. We have put angels into a separate thought chamber, as it were, and we do not allow them to enter our thoughts where they can encounter us in the only places they can encounter us in our day, for example, in our homes and in our places of work.

A scholar who was doing research on angels came to the conclusion that angels are older than God. Of course that cannot be, for nothing can be older than God. But they are older than the ideas the various religions have about their gods. In human language angels symbolize the fact that we are not alone on this earth, that we are visited by a higher power.

It is no wonder then that the angels have outlived the gods. They will outlive the religions as well. Angels have become a part of the language of modern man and will keep that place quite independently of any religious faith. As long as there are people in this world, those who have been overwhelmed by some remarkable change in their lives will find and use such words as "It was as if an angel came . . ." or "An angel passed this way" or "An angel watched over. . . ." People will be reminded of angels wherever they are overwhelmed by beauty, warmth, brilliance, and by words that seem to come from beyond this world.

Angels have a unique place in the Bible. They come and they go, but they are not here or there. We cannot lay hold of them by means of a mental picture or idea or doctrine. Our concepts are not adequate to grasp them. One angel story can call an angel a man while another calls him God. He can be one or several, visible or invisible; he can speak to us as one person speaking to another, or he can call down to us from heaven. Angels shatter our whole concept of substance, for they do not participate in substance. We can tell this from those stories in which angels hover, ascend, descend, speak from above, or are wafted off into the clouds.

One of the distinctions the Bible makes between God speaking and angels speaking is that everything God says stands in one context. But what is said of the angels is like the rising and waning of a shooting star across the night sky. Angels have no history, nor do they stand still in history. They come and go unexpectedly, linger for but a moment, then disappear without a trace. This shows again that angels are older than the gods. Angels belong to the time when there was no concept or writing of history, no systematic joining of time points in which life was experienced chiefly as a chain of moments which were the past in the full sense, a present which included a fulfilled past, and future. The Bible never tells a story about an angel who combines two points in time in what he says or does, that is, a story in which an angel would come again in order to fulfill what had been promised or to execute the judgment he had announced. On the contrary, however, the Bible's original confession of God is that what God says and does spans two points in time. God and history belong together, whereas the angel's sphere is solely the present. In the stories that tell about angels, the early era of humanity, along with its other experience of time, juts into a fullness of time.

In this respect, therefore, there have always been those periods that were especially sensitive to talk of angels or that dismissed such talk as nonsense. Most of the periods we call enlightened did not want to know anything about angels.

On the other hand, there have been times when there has been too much talk about angels, times in which speculation and doctrines about angels simply got out of hand. Such times were and are not times of fullness but rather times that created an unreal world. One such time was the period following the Babylonian exile; another, the Middle Ages.

Why Do You Ask My Name?

The two ways of access to God which determine the entire Bible, the worship and the name of God, that is, knowledge of God or theology, are forbidden to humankind as far as angels are concerned. The Bible wants to have nothing to do with angel worship or with doctrines about angels. Angels stand outside the realms of worship and theology.

This point becomes clear in two stories, one at the beginning, and one at the end of the Bible. In the first story, in Judges 13, an angel came to the wife of Manoah, who was childless, and told her that she would bear a child. Manoah asked the angel, "What is your name, so that, when your words come true, we may honor you?" The angel replied, "Why do you ask my name, seeing it is wonderful?" This conversation of the angel with the parents of Samson, who lived around 1100 B.C., is recorded in one of the oldest books of the Old Testament. It is peculiar, but certainly no accident, that in the later New Testament writings—Hebrews and Revelation—we find the same warning, the same rejection of angel worship. In the second story, in Revelation 19, the seer John, overwhelmed by the visions that had been given to him, wanted to prostrate himself before the angel who had shown him the visions: "Then I fell down at his feet to worship him, but he said to me, 'You must not do that. . . . Worship God.' "

These two stories are separated by a thousand years. Both demonstrate the inclination on the part of religious people to worship angels. But they also demonstrate very clearly that angel worship is prohibited. In the first story the prohibition involves the angel's refusal to give his name. Whoever knows an angel's name has, to a certain extent, control over him, knows him, and knows about him. So even this knowledge is forbidden.

What the Bible says about angels can be important for our time. Worship and theology today are in a crisis, and neither of these basic forms of relationships is exclusively Christian. Both have lost the acceptance with which they once were regarded to be an indispensable element of human societal life. Worship and theology (the doctrine of God) are wavering today between a harsh conservatism on the one hand and many a modern tendency toward dissolution on the other. The church buildings of this century are the best illustration of this wavering.

In the Bible, angels stand at the periphery of worship and theology, yet they belong to the Bible. Angels have a significance on the periphery which is not easy to recognize. They indicate the limits of both theology and worship. The Bible reports happenings and figures that can be comprehended neither by theology nor by worship. The stories of angels demonstrate that our speech cannot lay ahold of everything that God does and that our thoughts cannot manipulate God. These stories show us that all worship of God must accept the fact that there is a point where adoration (worship) and service cease, beyond which we are forbidden to go. But that is just the one delimiting side that angels in the Bible are supposed to communicate.

The One Who Encounters

The other side can be imagined if, in the many angel stories in the Old and New Testaments, one discerns a characteristic common to almost all of them. That characteristic is that the angel is the one who encounters. Most of the Bible's angel stories tell about an encounter. It is characteristic of these stories that the initiative lies solely with the angel. These encounters are like an unhoped-for visitation, for the one who is encountered by the angel is always taken by surprise. The Bible tells about angels because it wants to point to something that cannot be comprehended in the language of theology or in the rituals of worship. The stories of angels testify to still another means by which God encounters men and women.

What is an encounter? If we look at a person's lifeline from birth to death, we see the line of encounters detaching itself from the lifeline. In the very first and last moments of a human life there are no encounters. In the case of very young children the distance bridged is too insignificant; in the case of older people it has become too great—they are too far gone. The capacity for encounter within a human life is described by a curve that corresponds to but is not identical with the curve of creaturely life. Here there are risings, peaks, and declines depicting the capacity for encounter.

What is true for individuals is also largely true of human society. The encounter is varied among the eras of human history; it changes with the changes of societal forms and is itself a social occurrence of greatest finesse and sensitivity. Consequently, encounter has endless possibilities for change and accommodation.

In an early era, that which lives and encounters humans is not restricted to the circles of humankind. God can encounter humans, and so can messengers of God. An encounter with God is the exceptional, something that occurs only seldom. But precisely in the infrequency of this encounter with God there is something unmistakable: the most powerful expression of a direct encounter with God—prophecy. But the Old Testament knows another possibility: messengers of God can encounter anyone, without mistake and by surprise. That this once was so taken for granted and was not only believed but actually experienced, just like anything else we experience, is something to which the angel stories of the Bible constantly point. In those angel stories of an early period the angels do not come down from above; rather, they encounter men and women here on earth and in quite human ways. The angels in these stories encounter people just as one person encounters another. Later on, this kind of encounter undergoes a change. When we think of being encountered by an angel, we almost automatically think of the Christmas story, in which the angels appear to the shepherds. That is a rather late and infrequent sort of thing in the Bible, and it comes from the conflation of two entirely different occurrences that may under no circumstances be generalized, although it often is. No, in the old stories the most characteristic point is that the messengers of God encounter men and women here on earth in ordinary ways. In the moment of encounter they are not recognized as God's messengers. Therein lies the key to understanding the early stories of angels.

There is a story in the Old Testament which, for a brief moment, opens up to us that other world in which God's messengers really did encounter someone. That is the story in Genesis 18 of the three men who visited Abraham.

In the blazing noonday heat Abraham was sitting in the shade of his tent when he saw three travelers on the road nearby. He ran toward them and invited them to accept his hospitality. He offered them a festive meal and such comforts as his accommodations afforded. After the meal, Abraham received the message that his wife was to bear a child—and here it is only one who delivered the message.

The zeal with which Abraham served the three men, the insistence of his invitation, and the preparation of a festive meal were not for messengers of God. After all, how was Abraham supposed to know they were messengers of God? All these courtesies were for human guests.

There is no doubt that the intent of the story is to praise and commend hospitality. The lively portrayal presupposes in every sentence that the men hosted by Abraham were men who had the dust of the road on their feet, who knew what it was to be hungry and thirsty, and who were tired from their journeying. It is here that we stumble upon a world which has become alien to us, a world in which people expect that a messenger of God can come to them. What stands behind all Abraham's hospitality is the belief that when a stranger comes, it could be a messenger of God.

For the people of those days, and for a man like Abraham, the land in which they lived and roamed was strange and alien, and the only news that came was received from an occasional traveler, refugee, or messenger who came from a great distance. This distance was thought of as God's dwelling place. There was no fixed boundary between the distance from which a stranger came and that from which a messenger of God came, so one could always expect a messenger of God. Nor was there any question whether there were messengers of God; such a question simply could not arise. Now, angels here do not yet represent the transcendental world beyond, only a great distance. That is why they could encounter people along the road and that is why the people of Abraham's day, and even hundreds of years later, expected a visitation by a messenger of God.

There is quite a difference between this expectation and our modern belief in angels. What we today usually understand by "belief in angels" has almost nothing to do with the messengers of God in Abraham's day, or with the way the people of that day expected them. It could well be that every expectancy, as we see it in Abraham's hospitality and in the naturalness with which God's messengers were received in the Old Testament stories, needs an equivalent entirely different from a more or less strained belief in angels, which in our world has an entirely different meaning.

Here a New Testament context comes to mind. Jesus frequently and emphatically told his disciples that he would encounter them in the poor and needy and helpless. "Inasmuch as you have done it to the least of these my brethren, you have done it to me." Is this not an equivalent to the expectancy of Abraham, who extended hospitality to the three men because they could have been God's messengers? What a difference it would make in our social ministry if we really expected to encounter the messengers of the One who is beyond us in the persons of the helpless whom we encounter!

The Annunciation

In the famed Saint Lorenz Church in Nuremberg there is a large wood carving known as "The Annunciation." The carving depicts that moment when the angel came to Mary to tell her that she would give birth to a son. The angel's greeting to Mary has left a mark on the spiritual life of the West so pronounced that it is difficult to understand today. The Hail Mary is one of the most widely known prayers of Catholic piety. In his tract "On Translation," Luther tried to illustrate what he had in mind when he translated this into German as "Greetings to you, Mary, you blessed one. . . ."

Throughout the centuries the Annunciation has been portrayed repeatedly in works of art. From the Middle Ages to the present day the Hail Mary has been set to music by a host of composers. But that which is set to music or depicted visually is not something we can visualize from art or music. In the Bible there are two basic ways in which God reveals himself. One is by an epiphany, in which God shows himself as savior in the place of his people's need—for example, at the Red Sea, where they were threatened by the Egyptians, or else-where, where they were engaged in battle against the superior power of a foe. The other method God uses to reveal himself is theophany, by which he reveals himself in his majesty, usually in such natural phenomena as at Mount Sinai or, later, in the Temple, where he appeared to the prophet Isaiah as "high and lifted up." In both instances a greeting by God is simply unimaginable; it would be contrary to the situation immediately at hand.

If angels come to people with some kind of everyday greeting, then we can see in that a third manner of revelation, one quite different from the other two. In this third manner God becomes human in his messenger. We see this third manner of revelation in Jesus Christ, in whom the decisive event takes place here on earth, and in which act of revelation God's messenger leaves the sphere of the divine, the transcendental, in the moment when God's greeting is spoken.

The essential point hidden by the musical and other artistic portrayals of the Annunciation is that the angel's greeting is very much an everyday kind of greeting. This can be confirmed by looking at another story in which the angel's greeting is quite ordinary. Genesis 16 tells us that an angel had encountered Hagar, who had fled into the wilderness. The angel called her by name and asked her where she came from and where she was going.

The angel's question of whence and whither belongs very much to the realm of ordinary life among people who know each other and is asked in part out of common participation (as well as curiosity) in human life.

What is particularly drastic at this point is valid for angelic greetings in the Bible as a whole. Encounter with these messengers of God takes place not in a cultic, ecstatic, elevated sphere but far below, here, on the firm ground of everyday life. If we were not so accustomed to these angelic greetings, if they were not so elaborated upon and embroidered upon by the interpretations given them by artists, we would probably regard them as absurd and dismiss them, for the greeting is the specifically human, solely inner-human, event of contact which is confined to the realm of man. If someone greets me and I reply to that someone, I am accepting the person who greets me in the realm of my humanity. A greeting has immeasurable significance for human societal life. Existence in which there is no greeting ceases to be human. Greeting is a basic form of human speech. We see this quite clearly when we recognize how deeply rooted greeting is in our humanity, when we realize how it has been preserved through thousands of years, as far back as our knowledge of the human race can reach. We see also that the greeting is one of the very few forms of speech in which words and gestures go together everywhere in the world.

From all this, then, the meaning of the Annunciation becomes clear: it is the divine self-emptying, the incarnation of God, his descent into the human. One must imagine a world in which people believe themselves to be surrounded by super- and otherworldly forces, a world in which one reckons everyday with a manifold interaction of the otherworldly with the affairs of this

world. Such a world knows nothing of the enlighten-
ment of our day. In that world no one laughs or skep-
tically holds his tongue when someone openly says that
he has "seen the Lord, high and lifted up." One must try
to imagine what it meant in such a world when a messenger of God encountered a man or a woman with an
everyday, ordinary kind of greeting. The people in such
a world must have perceived the messengers of God as
realities over against themselves. For them the human
side of God's messenger was absolutely decisive. For
them the messenger of God was not a heavenly phenomenon but an earthly encounter.

The Angel's Departure

The supernatural nature of the angel was shown to people of biblical times not by an angel's coming but by his departure. One characteristic that is as frequent as the greeting at the beginning of an angel story is the angel's remarkable departure at the end.

In the story of the calling of Gideon we are told that the angel commanded Gideon to offer a sacrifice. Then with the tip of his staff the angel touched the meat and bread, causing fire to shoot from the rock and to consume the sacrifice. ". . . And the angel of the Lord vanished from his sight." Only then did Gideon realize that he had been speaking with a messenger of the Lord. The case is similar in the story of Samson's parents when an angel announced that a child was to be born. At the end of the story the Bible says: "And when the flame went up toward heaven . . . the angel of the Lord ascended in the flame of the altar while Manoah and his wife looked on." These two stories in Judges 6 and 13 bear a noticeable similarity to the New Testament story in Luke 24 of the disciples at Emmaus, in which their encounter with Jesus corresponds to the angel stories told in the Old Testament. Here Jesus joined himself to two of the disciples on the road, just like a messenger of God with Abraham or Gideon. In word and gesture the story is one of a human encounter right up to the very end when the stranger—Jesus—did something by which the disciples recognized him as one sent by God. With this Jesus vanished.

It is certainly noteworthy that the story of the walk to Emmaus tells us that at the outset the Lord joined the disciples as a traveler and was not recognized by his disciples. The story says that "their eyes were kept from recognizing him," but that after he performed the sign by which they recognized him "their eyes were opened." In the story of Hagar in Genesis 21 we are told that "God opened her eyes and she saw." Again, in connection with the story of Jacob's confrontation with the angel we are told in Genesis 33, "And Jacob lifted up his eyes." And in the story of Balaam in Numbers 22, "Then the Lord opened the eyes of Balaam." In the stories of Gideon and Samson in Judges 6 and 13 we have the recognition of the messenger of the Lord upon his departure. In each of these stories the angel left in a manner other than that in which he came. The eyes that beheld the angel's departure were not those that saw his coming. The decisive action took place between the angel's arrival and his departure: the eyes of those who had been visited were opened.

Let me try to illustrate my point from our situation. To be sure, the illustration is not the best, but at least it points in the direction in which we must look. Suppose we received a visit from a man who told us he had a certain matter about which he wanted to see us. And suppose he sat opposite us on a chair on which many others with similar matters had sat and on which many others would sit. We have an idea of what is on his mind, and our thinking is geared to what is to take place. Then something else takes place! The unexpected comes to us in his words. When the man gets up from his seat and we accompany him to the door and take our leave of him, a change has taken place like that of which we hear in the angel stories.

It is not really a question of whether we believe these stories in the Bible. Many will assume along with me that God no longer sends his messengers into the world as he sent them to Abraham and Gideon and others. The question is much more whether God can or cannot send his messengers in another way to a world and people that have changed so vastly over the centuries. Why should God not be able to do this? It depends very much on personal experience whether someone regards it as possible for such messengers to come into everyday life. There is a very pronounced difference between a person who has predetermined and fixed the day's messengers and visitors, and another person who in all the routine and pressure of work holds open the possibility that a message will come from elsewhere through a visitor, in a letter, or a phone call. Such a message will be one which, like that of the biblical angel stories, will open his eyes.

These stories of the comings and goings of messengers

of God show us that when they encounter men and women they are unrecognized. They come to us as human beings who belong here on earth, and their outward appearance does not identify them. It is only after their departure, when we look back upon their visitations, that can we say that messengers of God have come to us. An actual encounter with a messenger of God occurs only when the eyes of the person visited are opened, when the person visited recognizes the messenger of God in the changes that were brought about in his own life. No one whose eyes have not been opened by the message has seen the messenger. In the very moment that the messenger has done his duty, he is no longer there.

Now, having said all that, we have touched upon only a little of what the Bible has to say about angels. But even this little bit calls for considerable alertness. All these stories tell about the messenger of the Lord, one who brings a message, whose sole duty it was to make something known to a person and who is included in the story only for the sake of the message he communicated. The task of messenger of God later passed to that group of people we call prophets. It is not a coincidence that most stories of angelic messages are from the preprophetic period of the patriarchs and Judges, whereas the prophetic and historical books up to the time of the Babylonian exile have nothing to say about angelic messages. The fact that the Bible speaks in different ways in different periods about angels must make us extremely careful in the conclusions we draw from the

Bible and apply to our day and age. We cannot construct a timelessly valid doctrine of angels that is free from error.

But the few stories that tell about the messengers of God which have been handed down to us from early times show us what is essential and biblical in them quite apart from whatever else is to be heard from the Bible. In everything told us about angels of the Lord— from the messenger who came to Hagar to the one who came to Mary, the messenger who called Gideon to the angels at Christ's birth—we see they are undeniably in harmony with the goal of the Bible's entirety. The messenger of God cannot be written out of what the Bible reports.

The Servant of God

At this point I must remind the reader that the word *angel,* which in its real sense means messenger of God— what I have been talking about up to now—has become a collective concept that over the years has come to incorporate a mass of quite varied beings. The reader can best understand what follows by trying to look beyond this abstract summary and by being prepared to assume what cannot be justified in detail here, namely, that the servants of God, of whom we will now be speaking, originally had nothing to do with the messengers of God. To be sure, the subsequently generalized concept of angels has given a host of impulses to Western thought. But this generalized concept has clouded the essential evidence of the Bible.

Let me clarify this with an illustration. There is a painting by Andrea del Verrochio (ca. 1435–88) which hangs in London's National Gallery. The painting, "Tobias and the Angel on the Road," depicts a scene from the apocryphal Book of Tobias. It is a magnificent painting in which the artist took great pains to portray side by side the character of earthly and heavenly being. Young Tobias walks with full foot on the ground, but the angel walks on tiptoe. Now, whereas the garb of Tobias is contemporary and plain, the angel's garb is magnificent and of gold—a genuine fantasy costume. Between the two sets of clothing there is a fine line of distinction. The fluttering outer garment of Tobias suggests a unique likeness to angel's wings, so that in this pronounced distinction between a human being and a heavenly one there is a kind of aesthetic balance that makes their going side by side quite credible.

One senses in this painting how much Renaissance painters were wedded to the dogma of winged angels and to the general idea of angels whose attributes are fixed. Yet these painters also took issue with the problem that this fixed idea of what an angel looks like causes for the portrayal of historical events. In the Book of Tobias (around 200 B.C.) the angel has a number of recently acquired characteristics. But behind these characteristics is the ancient and basic theme of the messenger of God in which the unrecognized angel joins himself to Tobias as man to man. The idea of an angel with wings is unthinkable in the story of Tobias. In Verrochio's painting the angel even has a halo. One can see that right up to the Renaissance the figure of a winged angel—the wings identifying the angel as a heavenly being, a fantasy figure—dominated the thinking of Christendom even to the point that paintings actually contradicted the story the painting sought to portray. There could hardly be a clearer demonstration that the Western idea of angels is not faithful to the Bible. The messenger of God who approaches people in a human manner, who greets them and joins them along the way and is recognized as a messenger of God who opens their eyes only when the angel has departed, has absolutely nothing to do with those winged beings we call angels.

These winged creatures, however, are to be found outside the Bible and the Christian religion, but they do not belong to the Bible or to Christianity. This can be seen immediately just by a glance at Persian art. On Persian miniatures dating from the time of the Book of Tobias we find figures of creatures which correspond to the Christian mental image of angels. There we find a figure of a winged angel hovering in the air which dates back to the fourth century before Christ. This kind of portrayal of an angel has about it absolutely nothing that is specifically Christian, but it can be traced back to mental images of mixed beings which are thousands of years old, especially those found in depictions of Egyptian deities and of the deities of other religions as well.

In the context of that of which I have been speaking belong also the cherubim and seraphim, as well as the heavenly hosts, of which the Bible speaks. These heavenly beings, called *bene elohim*, or the sons of the gods, are mentioned in several places in the Bible. According to Gen. 6:1–4 these sons of the gods married women, and from their union sprang the race of giants. Here a piece of pre-Israelitic myth intrudes into biblical history and shows us, in a way that is typical of the whole Bible, that these heavenly beings come to us out of the distant past of preceding religions and are a kind of bridge between the Bible and those other religions.

In the Old Testament we encounter these heavenly beings as servants who surround the throne of God. Even though it depicts them as such, the Bible had no real interest in these figures. They simply serve to portray the majesty of God. In the call of the prophet Isaiah (6:1–3) we read:

> I saw the Lord sitting upon a throne, high and lifted up; and his train filled the temple. Above him stood the seraphim; each had six wings: with two he covered his face, and with two he covered his feet, and with two he flew. And one called to another and said: "Holy, holy, holy is the Lord of hosts; the whole earth is full of his glory."

This impressive description can give us the best idea of what meaning these heavenly beings who surrounded the throne of God had for that time. A century before Isaiah, another prophet had a similar vision of God's throne surrounded by servants (1 Kings 22). The same scene is portrayed in Job 1 and 2, in Zech. 6:5, in several psalms, and in the baroque visions of Ezekiel. These heavenly beings serve God (Job 4:18; Ps. 104:4), execute his commands (Zech. 6:5), and praise and worship him (Ps. 103:20–21; 148:1–2; Isa. 6:3). All this is intended to do nothing but declare the majesty of God. Behind such talk there is a thoroughly human, one might well say primitive, idea of lordship. For thousands of years humankind could not conceive of lordship in any other way than by picturing a lord sitting upon a throne, surrounded by servants who are there to execute his commands but at the same time are the living reflection of his absolute power. This form of lordship, in which the lord does absolutely nothing but sit peacefully and give commands that his servants carry out, did not always exist. That kind of lordship reflects a settled society as opposed to a nomadic one. In fact, this is the form of lordship we picture and have pictured for several thousand years. But in our time we find that this image is beginning to change. In place of a lord's direct, personal command we visualize the kind of lordship that is increasingly exercised through mechanical devices and, instead of through servants (department heads or cabinet ministers) who surround the throne, through technological devices and bureaucracy.

When the Israelites, after their settlement of the Promised Land, wanted to portray the majesty of God, the most natural way was to depict him as seated upon a throne surrounded by his servants. But the essential difference in such portrayals is whether the emphasis is upon God the Lord or upon the heavenly beings. We see that in the early period (i.e., up to the Babylonian exile) one could speak without embarrassment about God's heavenly realm and the servants who surrounded his throne without these servants as such being important. In the entire prophecy of Isaiah there is no further mention of seraphim or other heavenly beings. They have just one purpose: to bear witness to the majesty of God. After the Babylonian exile, however, the situation became quite different because God had become more remote from his people, more transcendent. At this point in history the heavenly beings as such became both more important and interesting. We see the entire realm of angels begin to unfold in the visions of Ezekiel and Zechariah. We see a kind of intermediary world between God and man come into being. In the course of this development the heavenly beings received their own unique, fixed areas of responsibility; they received names and were brought into relationships with each other. Over the rank-and-file angels were the archangels, and thus a whole hierarchy developed which has come down to Protestant Christianity, even into the hymnbooks. At the end of this development are the late Jewish apocryphal writings, which offer a detailed and fully developed doctrine of angels, for example, the Book of Enoch. But even the canonical Book of Daniel presupposes a developed doctrine of angels, much of which was taken over by the New Testament.

It is not difficult to understand how the simple portrayal of God sitting as Lord upon a throne and surrounded by his servants developed into the hierarchies of angels of the later period. The development is parallel to the development and distinction of the exercise of power among humankind. Even the kings of this earth have not remained surrounded by servants who carry out their commands. These servants or cabinet ministers received specific functions. In due course these functionaries had to have their own servants in order to carry out their increasing number of duties. And so it went on until a regular hierarchy of nobility— of which we have remnants down to the present day—

grew up among these servants of God. The same thing happened with these servants of God in Israel's later period. Here it can be said that the creation of an entire realm and hierarchy of angels was something spun out of fantasy and speculation. The extensive doctrine of angels of the later period is not something that was simply dreamed up. In this development there can be found a large number of motives that have their origins in other religions. A great many polytheistic characteristics found their way into the doctrine of angels and thereby into the faith of the later period of Israel, whose fundamental confession was that God is one. We see here the same thing we see in the history of the early and high medieval period of the Christian church: the difficulty of maintaining the faith in one God, the belief that apart from him no one and nothing can be designated, understood, or worshiped as God.

That there is danger even in talk about these divine beings, these servants of God who surround his throne and do his will, if such talk is entirely unconscious and not really interested in these beings is seen with particular clarity in the priestly version of the Book of Genesis, which does not mention angels at all. To this book belongs the story of creation. Here there is but a barely audible suggestion of the servants who surround the throne of God in the plural form in which God speaks his intention, "Let us make man. . . ."

Thus does the King speak to his environment. The old idea of God's court-state is still in the background, but it is faded and distant. God's work no longer requires servants to carry out his commands. He speaks, and his word is fulfilled. The priestly writing received its final form during the time of the Babylonian exile or shortly thereafter. This is the same period in which—especially in the case of Ezekiel and, somewhat later, Zechariah—interest in heavenly beings so increased that a fully developed doctrine of angels developed. In the postexilic period there were two types of piety. One type leaned heavily toward angels and their work; the apocalyptic literature is the best example of this. The other type of piety rejected all belief in angels. That holds true also for the New Testament period with respect to the position of the Sadducees, who denied the existence of angels.

What the Bible has to say about angels has another aspect that is interesting for our day. Ps. 104:3–4 says: ". . . who makest the clouds thy chariot, who ridest on the wings of the wind, who makest the winds thy messengers, fire and flame thy ministers." Even the stars can be spoken of as God's servants (see Job 38:7). The stars, clouds, winds, and lightning are God's servants. They await his bidding, carry out his commands, and praise and glorify him. It seems clear that in that kind of talk there are echoes of a polytheistic faith which can be recognized and in which all these natural phenomena were of a divine sort to be looked upon as personal. The star deities here are demoted to being servants of the one living God, as are the clouds, winds, and weather. It is possible that the cherubim of the Old Testament originally were poeticized storm clouds. In the old epiphanies God rode upon such clouds; in other places he rode upon a cherubim. The very name cherubim suggests its foreign origin; it is related to the Babylonian word *kuribu*. The same picture is encountered in other religions. The Indian deity Vishnu rides upon a *garuda*, which probably corresponds to the Greek *gryps* (Latin, *gryphus*; English, *griffin*).

The natural forces deified by other religions here become servants of the God who created heaven and earth. This aspect of speaking in the Bible of the forces of nature as servants of God receives a special meaning for humanity, which has made and continues to make the forces of nature into its servants. If the Bible understood the forces of nature which were known at that time as servants of God, that presumes that humankind can never have complete control over those forces. Even those forces of nature which have been subdued, harnessed, and utilized remain servants of God. That holds also for those forces such as electricity, and the power derived from the splitting of the atom, which have been recognized by humankind. Basically nothing else is there. A person's ability to subject the earth's forces to oneself is as limited today as it was long ago by the lordship of God, who makes the winds his messengers and the flames of fire his servants. But that does not say that the harnessing of atomic power is reprehensible, nor that it is something contrary to God's plan for his creation. To be sure, we shall have to develop very concrete and effective economic and social forms to express God's lordship over the forces over which we have gained control. In any case, what the Bible has to say about the forces of nature as servants of God can make us certain that whatever changes there may be in humankind's relationship to those forces, they are not outside God's action. It is to be regretted that over the last two centuries the word of God has not been applied effectively to these new realms, and that the church's preaching has followed this development only with great difficulty and almost exclusively in a critical vein. Psalm 148 is a summons to all creation to praise the creator. It calls first of all upon angels to praise him, then upon sun, moon, stars, and all that is created in heaven and on earth. Even in this psalm the forces of creation are designated as servants of God: ". . . fire and hail, snow and frost, stormy wind fulfilling his command." To press this call upon creation to praise the creator, to extend these lines to the forces unleashed in our world and to the ways of humankind in the world in which we live—that is one of the tasks of theology in our time!

Angels That Accompany
and Protect

The guardian angel occupies a unique place between the "angel of God" and the heavenly beings that are God's servants. Everything the Bible says about the guardian angel can be said about God himself. It is not necessary to speak about a guardian angel. It is always God himself who acts through the guardian angel. One has only to read the beautiful story of the courtship of Rebekah in Genesis 24 to see this. When Abraham dispatched his servant he said, "He will send his angel before you." Upon his arrival the servant prostrated himself and praised the Lord who had accompanied him and led him along the right path. The one who accompanies can be God himself as well as an angel, and the same story can speak first of one and then of the other. The same is true of the messenger of God, upon whose place and in whose stead God himself can enter in the very middle of a story. This alternating between the two is characteristic of what the Bible has to say about the guardian angel. It is the intention of the Bible not to provide a special figure apart from and in addition to God but rather to emphasize God's care for what is endangered and unprotected in particular proximity to a person. This care of God can best be understood by talking about an angel. In the promise of protection (Psalm 91) through an angel there is something difficult to define: "For he will give his angels charge of you to guard you in all your ways."

When we talk about guardian angels, especially in children's songs, it is not by accident. Nor is it a matter of making belief in angels something "cute," for it is precisely with children that the guardian, protecting angel has his special task. We can speak of a guardian angel only with respect to a certain period of childhood. The reason for this is found in the prehistory of belief in guardian angels. It goes back so far into the very earliest stages of humanity that we can see and understand the relationship to God which we see in it as something we can only call childlike. The belief that an individual had a personal god or goddess, or both, is an offshoot of this ancient belief. In Egyptian, Sumerian, and Babylonian religion this personal god or goddess was in addition to the major deities to whom all were subject. A great Sumerian poem speaks of these deities:

> He [the god] turns man's song to joy;
> He gave man the good spirit
> As watchman and guard,
> Gave him the protecting spirits
> Who were most friendly to him.

In some religions the belief in protecting spirits developed out of the idea of an external soul that can detach itself from the body and become a personal guardian spirit. For example, in Germanic religion these were the Fylgjur (Wagner's *Valkyrie*), the Fravashis of Parsism, the guardian angels of postexilic Judaism. This belief was especially pronounced in Egyptian religion, which believed that one received a *ka* (often depicted in the form of a bird) that then accompanied one throughout his entire life, a double so to speak. Quite often the spirits of the dead had the function of a guardian angel or an announcing angel (e.g., among the pygmies of Central Africa). The common element in all these religions is the personal good spirit assigned to each mortal. But a sharp distinction cannot be made between spirit, god, or angel. The essential element of all this is a knowledge that reaches out from the earliest stages of the human race that each individual human being is hidden and surrounded by one who belongs to that individual alone, and who means him only well.

Understood in this way, the deeply rooted belief in a guardian, accompanying angel could come to a new and undreamed-of meaning. One fact which cannot be denied is that in people of our day, who have been caught up in the devilish ways of destroying individual existence, this belief in a personal guardian angel, with all its simplicity and childlike power, is reawakened. A great many people who would never talk about this belief have nonetheless sung and prayed the old morning and evening hymns and prayers that speak of the protection of angels. In these poems and prayers the protecting angel is no longer a figure passed down by tradition or concocted by fantasy, but a living reality. Precisely in the early stories of the Bible we again encounter what characterizes our talk about angels, in particular the guardian and accompanying angels. When one of these angels speaks, he speaks of God.

> Of those good powers wonderfully hidden
> We await in faith whate'er may come
> God is with us at evening and at morning
> Most surely at the break of each new day.
> —Bonhoeffer

Angels and Jesus Christ

If someone were to ask what the New Testament has to say about angels and what part they have in it, a single glance would offer a peculiar discovery. The New Testament speaks emphatically about angels only in three places: in connection with Jesus' birth, with his leaving this earth, and with his coming again. These three points contain the basic answer to such a question.

For one thing, the answer shows us that the New Testament has no more of a doctrine about angels than does the Old Testament. Nowhere does the message of Jesus or the exposition of that message in the letters of the apostles have angels at the center. Christ did not come to reveal anything about angels. The message of Jesus can be taught and preached without saying one thing about angels. Nonetheless, the New Testament does speak of angels, although only peripherally, and it speaks of them with a degree of emphasis only in the passages mentioned earlier. What meaning, then, do they have for the New Testament?

ANGELS AT THE BIRTH OF JESUS

The context of the stories dealing with the birth of Christ can be compared to the very early stories about the angel of God in the Old Testament. There the message of God concentrated on two particular situations: the need of childless women, in which case the impending birth of a child is announced, and the announcement to men of salvation from the oppression of society. Both these motifs come together in the angelic message at the beginning of the Gospel of Luke. We have already seen that the message the angel delivered to Mary is essentially like that delivered to Hagar in Genesis 16. If in the announcement of the angels to the parents of John the Baptist and of Jesus, and in the announcement to the shepherds, the basic needs of men and women are heard and a turning point is promised with the birth of the Savior of the world, then the meaning of these stories dealing with the birth of Christ becomes clear. In the stories of Christ's birth we find the fulfillment of what men and women for thousands of years have awaited, hoped, and begged for. The announcement of salvation that came to Mary, as it came to Abraham, Hagar, and Gideon, in a human greeting, will become human for all in the man Jesus Christ. That announcement will be able to confront all in a human way, for Jesus as a human being speaks the message, the good news, to the sick and lowly, and he helps them. When this Jesus of Nazareth brings what he has to bring not only to men but to women and children as well, there merged together in him what the people of the Old Testament believed about the messenger of God who came to them where they were, to men, women, and children in their need, to protect them.

ANGELS AT THE RESURRECTION

In connection with what has been said above, the stories about the Resurrection (see Matt. 28:2ff.; Mark 16:5ff.; Luke 23:4ff.; John 20:12ff.; and also the Transfiguration account in Matthew 17 and par.), in which angels confront us, become more understandable. We have already pointed out the great similarity of the story of the walk to Emmaus to the angel stories of the Old Testament. In these stories we found the essential characteristic in the difference between the angel's coming and his departure. Like those messengers of God, Christ directed his message to people where they were and in their language. He was in every way a human being like us. Only in his departure did it become apparent who he is. As it had been said of the messengers of God, so was it said of him, that he vanished before their very eyes. The reason what the Gospels say about Christ's departure from this earth corresponds to the account of his Incarnation is that in Christ, God's action has touched this earth totally and completely. Consequently that line of angel stories is picked up in which the messenger of God comes like a human being, and it is only at his departure that it is recognized where he belongs. The meaning of the angels in the Resurrection stories is to point to the other homeland of the man Jesus of Nazareth. Angels could not be absent from the Gospels; they are a constituent element of the report of what happened in and through Jesus Christ.

Still another characteristic of the angel stories finds its way into the Resurrection narratives: the eyes of those to whom the messenger came were opened at his departure. Some of the pertinent passages are indicated above. Of the disciples at Emmaus it was said, "And their eyes were opened." That those whom the messenger of God encountered were changed by the encounter is part and parcel of the whole event reported. The ones who were changed were the ones who saw the departure of God's messenger. This departure is not an objective fact that can be tested, proved, and made accessible to every observer. It cannot be separated from the totality, that is, from the mission of the messenger and the message itself, and be examined and discussed by itself.

The same is also true of Jesus' Resurrection. The Resurrection is not an isolated act that can be analyzed and observed by itself. It is not a miracle that happened after the death of Jesus of Nazareth, something one can take up by itself and fit into some context. Just as the Resurrection is the other side of Christ's coming to this earth, so it is also the witness of those who have been changed by the encounter with the messenger. No one can honestly say that the Lord is risen who at the same time does not say, "Did not our hearts burn within us?"

ANGELS AT THE LORD'S COMING AGAIN

If we related the angel stories of the Old Testament to the references to angels in the New Testament in connection with Christ's coming to and departure from this earth, then all these stories would deal exclusively with the angel of God, with God's messenger who came to a woman or a man to announce something or to accompany or protect them. As for the other angels, the servants of God who are usually spoken of in the plural and stand about his throne to serve and praise him, they are spoken of almost exclusively in connection with the Lord's coming again.

This fact is basic to understanding what the New Testament has to say about angels. What the New Testament says about the angels of God, what it takes up from the Old Testament and declares to be fulfilled, is firmly tied to the way of Christ on earth. But the heavenly beings, the servants of God, fade into the background of Jesus' ministry on earth; we hear almost nothing of them. The New Testament speaks of angels as heavenly beings who are part of the portrayal of God's majesty, and it confines what it has to say about angels almost exclusively to the Lord's coming again at the end of history. In view of this fact it is clear that in the New Testament the general concept "angel" embraces a variety of things that have varied roots. The messengers of God at Jesus' birth and Resurrection are essentially different from the angels who will accompany the Son of man when he returns at the end of history (Matt. 25:31; 26:27) and who will then gather the elect (Matt. 24:31; Mark 13:27) and pass judgment on the lost (Matt. 13:39ff.). (See Paul in this connection in 1 Thess. 4:16; 2 Thess. 1:7.) The sole purpose of speaking of angels in this connection is to point to another reality which is over against ours, for which all our criteria and concepts and mental images no longer suffice. Here, then, is a clear distinction between what the Old Testament says about the servants of God and what the New Testament says. What can be seen in the Old Testament (as was typical of the thinking of the times) in essentially spatial terms—God's throne in his heavenly realm, surrounded by his servants—is seen by the New Testament, if not entirely, yet more emphatically, in terms of time. As the New Testament sees it, when Christ returns, the heavenly legions, the servants of God who are also servants of the exalted Lord, receive their significance for the last act of the drama of the history of salvation.

It is only in this matter, solely in view of the Lord's coming again, that we can observe the New Testament's special interest in angels which—and in this respect it corresponds to the Old Testament—becomes very pronounced in later writings. In the Gospels, angels are mentioned only in connection with Christ's coming again, but the Book of Revelation paints a broader picture of them. In Revelation—as in the case of the apocalyptic writings of postexilic Judaism—there is an entire realm populated by angels. Here we encounter all kinds of messengers and servants of God, powerful and dreadful spirits. The first verse of Revelation speaks of the angel who interpreted the visions to John. This angel is encountered throughout the book and is often referred to as the angel who had spoken to John (Rev. 21:15). The seven letters to the seven churches are all preceded by the injunction "And to the church in . . . write. . . ."

The angels mentioned in connection with these churches can probably be traced back to the patron angels of the people. According to Jewish thought discernible in the Old Testament, especially in Daniel, every race and people has an angel which mediates between it and God. In Daniel this guardian and mediating angel is named Michael, and we also find him in the Revelation of John.

In Revelation the old idea of God's heavenly court and the angels who surround his throne plays a particularly important role. Even in the salutation that John extends to the congregations these angels are mentioned: ". . . and from the seven spirits who are before his throne. . . . " John hears the "voice of many angels" standing about the throne (Rev. 5:11), praising God and Christ. The entire Book of Revelation resounds with the praise of angels (chaps. 5, 8, 10, 19). These angels are also God's servants who, at his command, carry out the drama of the Last Judgment, the ending and changing of all things. It is they who sound the trumpets of judgment. It is an angel that comes down from heaven and, setting one foot on the firmament and the other in the sea, calls out so that the thunders reply to him. The angel's are God's army; under Michael's leadership they wage war against the dragon (Revelation 12). Angels of judgment pour out the bowls of God's wrath (Revelation 15), and an angel binds Satan with chains (Revelation 20). Twelve angels stand guard at the gates of the new Jerusalem and from above an angel announces the fall of Babylon (Revelation 18). Further, an angel summons the birds of the air to feast on the corpses from the great and final battle. When all is said and done, the entire Book of Revelation could be described as a drama of angels. From first to last the angels are the actors.

Here something needs to be said quite clearly about the abundance of Revelation's portrayal of angels. We must refrain from trying to derive from its faltering attempts at pointing to the boundaries of history any kind of doctrine or teaching about angels which would bind the consciences of humankind for all times and places. That this is the intention of the Bible's final book and of its author is demonstrated at the end of the book. John wants to fall down before the angel who has shown him all his visions. The angel responds, "You must not do that. . . . Worship God."

It is quite clear that preoccupation with angels, their being, and what they can do can lead to a veneration of angels. But it cannot be said more clearly than is said at the end of Revelation that the Bible wants no part of such a veneration of angels; indeed, it even forbids it. The same is true of other passages in the New Testament. The first two chapters of Hebrews go into great detail to emphasize that Christ is exalted above the angels. Angels are "serving spirits" especially in the service of the Gospel (Heb. 1:14). In Revelation (19:10; 22:8–9) they are called fellow servants. In the writings of Paul we find a number of statements that speak to this subject (esp. Gal. 1:8; 2 Cor. 11:4; Rom. 8:38; 1 Cor. 6:3). Col. 2:18 specifically rejects the veneration of angels.

When one takes into consideration how belief in

angels grew by leaps and bounds in Judaism during the Hellenistic period, it must be said that the New Testament broke through the entire wasteland of speculation to a modest, simple, and reverent way that is completely centered in God's acts. Never—except in Revelation—is there any mention of angels solely for the sake of angels; only rarely—and at that unconsciously— does a line of postexilic belief in angels slip over into the New Testament. Our example of this is in the passages Acts 7:53 and Gal. 3:19, which speak of the Law being mediated to Israel through an angel. The overwhelming attitude of the New Testament over against all speculation about and veneration of angels is critical and admonitory. This attitude of the New Testament is also expressed in the Old Testament with respect to the peculiar function of an angel.

The Mediating Angel

The preexilic prophets received the words they were to proclaim directly from God. Precisely how they received those words will remain forever a secret, but at least it is clear that these words could not have been given by beings whose function was to transmit them. The prophet heard what he was to proclaim directly from God.

The Babylonian exile changed that situation. Ezekiel was the first prophet to encounter an angel who mediated between him and God and communicated what the prophet was to preach. The function of this angel is especially clear in Ezekiel's vision of the new temple (Ezekiel 40–48). The beginning of Ezekiel 40 is very similar to the beginning of the Book of Revelation. Ezekiel, too, is caught up in the spirit and beholds a "man" who addresses him, "Son of man, look with your eyes, and hear with your ears, and set your mind upon all that I shall show you. . . ."

And, as in Revelation, Ezekiel was commanded to make known to the house of Israel all that he would see.

If we compare the two passages we will see that the beginning of Revelation is patterned along the lines of Ezekiel 40. Here, too, the mediating angel has his origin. This talk about a mediating angel becomes more pronounced and frequent in the prophecy of Zechariah. Here the mediating angel who spoke to the prophet is the constant and indispensable mediator and clarifier. In Zechariah this angel is mentioned some seventeen times, and here the designation "mediating" is most intimately associated with the prophet's vision (Zech. 1:8–9):

> I saw in the night, and behold, a man riding upon a red horse! He was standing among the myrtle trees in the glen. . . . Then I said, "What are these, my lord?" The angel who talked with me said to me, "I will show you what they are."

And so it goes in Zechariah from one nocturnal vision to another. The seer has a vision, but he stands helplessly before it, much like a foreigner in a land whose language he does not understand. Again and again he needs someone who understands the language of supernatural visions to explain them to him in a language he understands.

The same is true of the visions in Daniel. In chapter 7 the visions of Daniel are described, and he is deeply troubled because he cannot understand them (Dan. 7:16): "I approached one of those who stood there and asked him the truth concerning all this. So he told me. . . ." Running through Ezekiel, Daniel, and Zechariah is the same course of events found in the Book of Revelation—in each case the angel has the function of interpreting the human seer's visions. If, then, in all these passages the course of events is the same and the meaning of the angels is the same, then this is an indication that there is an especially pronounced and fixed idea we must pursue.

What is the meaning of this mediating angel? In each of these books this angel is clearly distinct from the heavenly beings, the actors in a supernatural drama whom the seer sees in his visions. This angel stands at the prophet's side and interprets what the seer sees. Basically he corresponds to the messenger of God of early times. Out of that messenger evolved the interpreter. The distinction is seen when we compare this angel with the messenger of God in the early stories. He is no longer the one here on earth who meets people along the road. Rather, he belongs to that mysterious world seen in the vision. The angel is there with the vision, he belongs to it, and then he stands at the seer's side to interpret what the seer beholds. He is, as it were, a figure who steps out of the drama and mediates between the vision and human reality.

In the Bible this mediating angel is a sign that God has become remote from humankind. The angel stands in a place to which a door has been closed, namely, where the direct hearing of God's word has ceased. This is true in both Testaments. Seen historically, the mediating angel is encountered at the point where preexilic prophecy came to an end. The epochal transformation of prophecy to apocalyptic runs throughout Ezekiel. In his vision of the new temple, Ezekiel has become an apocalyptist. With this transition Zechariah goes even further. In Daniel, apocalypticism has replaced prophecy completely. At this point God is so remote that his word can no longer be heard directly. With this change of circumstance, the apocalyptic vision took the place of the word that the prophet heard. It is clear to those who behold such a vision that they no longer have the directness of a word of God to a mortal. The seer can be quite deeply shaken by what he sees, but he can no longer understand it. He stands helplessly before the unfolding visions of supernatural forms and dramas and does not know what they mean. The mediating angel who interprets the vision stands in the place of the descendants of the prophets, who no longer have the word of God spoken directly to them. All apocalypse—even with explanation provided by the mediating angel—hovers in that mysterious, incomprehensible world in between. Even the angel's explanation does not change the fact that the directness of hearing is no longer there.

How did it happen that the apocalyptists needed the explanation of an interpreter? One thing is clear: the time of prophecy, the direct hearing and speaking of God's word through those messengers we call prophets, was quite limited. It was coterminous with the kingdom from the first kings of Israel and Judah to the last. That is the side of a series of events we can see and fix historically. There is, however, another side to this course of events. Throughout this period the prophets had primarily declared to the people God's judgment. Above all else they were messengers of the judgment to come. That judgment was fulfilled in the collapse of Israel and Judah, the destruction of Jerusalem and the Temple. This consummation of the judgment had a deep and transforming effect upon the remnant. They affirmed the justness of the judgment that had befallen them and with it the accumulated guilt of generations. The result of this transformation was that their God, the God of their fathers, the God of judgment and justice, became so majestic, so otherworldly, for them that there could never again be a direct hearing of God's word. They were convinced that their God still directed the course of history. But direct access to God's acting in history was no longer attainable. God was too far removed.

It is precisely this that gave shape and substance to the mediating angel. These prophets, in their total dedication, looked into the darkness of history and knew that God continued to act. They saw God's acting in visions that shook them to the foundations of their being. But they could not understand what they saw. That door was closed to them. Only one who belonged to God's realm could give them entry. So, then, the mediating angels corresponded to the angels of God stationed at the Garden of Eden following the expulsion of Adam and Eve. The kingdom of God had to be closed to the disobedient. This course of events continued from Israel's beginning to its collapse in disobedience, and ultimately to the destruction of the nation and the

Babylonian exile. Just as direct human contact with God ceased with the expulsion from Eden, so did God's direct communication with the prophets. God had withdrawn into the distance. Even though the apocalyptist's mediating angel revealed to him the meaning of what he saw, the visions remained, and direct access to God was still not available.

Something quite different entered the world with the coming of Christ, something of which we sing

> This day he opens wide the gate
> To Paradise once more;
> The cherub bars no more the way;
> To God be laud and praise!

In Christ the directness that was lost is restored. When the entire New Testament calls Jesus of Nazareth the Son of God, it means that the directness which had been lost is restored. Jesus did not need visions to know what the Father expected of him and wanted him to do: "I and the Father are one." The Gospel of John especially is full of Jesus' direct access and immediacy to God (esp. John 5:17ff.), and this excludes any kind of mediating between him and God. Unlike the apocalyptic seer, Jesus does not stand before a closed door. He does not need a mediating angel because he himself is the one who mediates the Father's words: "I declare to the world what I have heard from him" (John 8:26). In him is the fulfillment of that message which has come from God to his people. The position of mediating, interpreting angel ceases to exist.

The church has not always recognized this fact. If the mediating angel as we meet him in the postexilic apocalyptic writings reappears in the Revelation of John, the revelation thus received, like the corresponding Old Testament revelations, can claim only a temporally limited validity. The world of angels in John's Revelation simply cannot be added to that which Jesus of Nazareth received directly from his Father without angelic mediation. The door to the heavenly realm is opened no farther by the mediating angel than by the coming of the Son.

But the cessation of the mediating angel's mission because direct access to God is restored has considerable significance beyond that. Over the centuries, an institution of the church has taken the place of the mediating angel who interprets. When the church speaks of an infallible teaching office, an institution of the church, a human institution, is elevated to a position to which it has no right. This infallible teaching office stands in the place of the mediating angel, where God's direct speaking to humans is no more; it is the counterpart to that mediating angel who interprets the seer's visions to him. There is a distinction, however, in that the seers of the Bible, without exception, admit their inability to interpret the visions by themselves. We cannot restrict this unjustified continuation of the mediating angel to the Roman Catholic church and to what it holds to be—with certain limitations—the infallible teaching office. Even in Protestant churches such a teaching has been taken so for granted and has been so absolutized that it has come dangerously close to being a "mediating angel."

Such a teaching led to the use of this mediating-angel idea to replace the directness of God's speaking to humankind, which had been restored with a new kind of mediatorship. Any kind of theology that lays claim to autonomy—between Christ and his people, between Christ and the world—and to its own realm, rules, language, and authority is not the kind that follows Christ, the kind in which the message of the Old Testament is fulfilled. We no longer need a mediating, interpreting angel, or a replacement for him, because Christ has come. The theology of Christ's church can only be an exposition of what is said to us, a bearing of witness to the attestation of the messengers who have seen what has come to pass. Neither theology nor the church's officeholders are as exalted above earthly reality as the mediating angels who, from their position, could see more than earthly seers. Even Christ did not remain in that mediating state. Rather, he came entirely and wholly down to us, where we are, where the word of the Savior can confront us all.

A Final Word

In this book we have been considering those stories of the Bible which tell about angels. But we have not been able to define what an angel is—what his nature, shape, or mission is. Indeed, our conclusion is that angels cannot be defined. Where we find them in the Bible they point to the limitation of our thought, our imagination, and our ability to conceptualize.

The Bible does not speak uniformly about the angels. Actually, the idea of angels is a collective concept that was formulated at a later date and embraces a variety of things. For one thing, from beginning to end of the Bible there is a distinction between "the angel of God," the messenger who comes bearing a message from God for an individual, and the servants of God, who surround God's throne and represent his majesty. Then there is the second interval, extending from the early period, in which we can speak of the "angel of God" as though we were speaking of an appearance of God himself, to a later time, in which it was believed that there was a separate and vast kingdom of angels between God and humankind.

Moreover, we have seen that the stories and contexts which speak of angels with restraint and in a way that points to something say and can mean more to us than the apocalyptic writings at the end of the Old and New Testament eras. In these writings we see the development of an entire "world in between" which is inhabited by angels, which leads us on a detour of speculation and fantasy about angels, something against which the Bible itself warns. If, then, the Bible in both Old and New Testaments accepted these broad portrayals of angels, the important thing for us is that we be shown the limitations of the reality we see, that we recognize that the kingdom of God embraces more than we can see or know.

The angel stories in the Bible confront us not so much with the question of whether we believe in angels but with the question of whether we believe that they quietly summon us to be ready for God's messages. How these messages come to people is for God alone to say. These messages need not come tomorrow as they came yesterday. But the angels of whom the Bible speaks are an unmistakably ineradicable code for the fact that we mortals on the pathways of this earth and in the houses we have built are not alone; we are visited.

The story of all God's messages is fulfilled in Jesus Christ, in whom God has visited and redeemed his people. But the fact that Christ came does not mean that God has stopped sending his messages to us here on earth.